Freedom
of the
News Media

ALSO BY OLGA G. AND EDWIN P. HOYT
Censorship in America

BY EDWIN P. HOYT
The Palmer Raids, 1919–1920

FREEDOM OF THE NEWS MEDIA

by Olga G. and Edwin P. Hoyt

THE SEABURY PRESS · NEW YORK

CONTENTS

Freedom of the News Media

INTRODUCTION

Late in 1969 and on into the early 1970s the Nixon administration quarreled with a press that had never been particularly friendly to it. Out of the quarrel arose a series of statements and acts by political figures and media representatives
that brought into question the whole situation of the American press in the second half of the twentieth century.

After the initial smoke had cleared away, two questions remained: Was there serious threat to freedom of the media in
the United States? Was the press—and this meant the electronic as well as the printed media—acting responsibly or ir-
responsibly? This book focuses on these two basic questions.

There are many peripheral questions, of course. They
begin with the negative attitudes of various reporters and
publications toward the Nixon administration, wherein all
the hubbub began. But to understand these attitudes and to
judge them, one must go back to the beginnings and examine other attitudes of the American press at other times.
Then there is the politician's attitude toward the press. Was
Vice President Spiro Agnew justified in criticizing a large
segment of the press for bias? What was the performance record of the press in previous times? Could an administration
bear down on the press and threaten it successfully? Had this
ever been done before, and had the press been muzzled?
Again, history holds the answers to such questions.

There were new elements in the 1970s. Television had come to the fore as the single most important medium of information in the nation. How well was it performing? Here again, history is important to an understanding of where the medium of television is today. The history of radio, too, is important because radio is the parent of electronic journalism and in the 1970s was still an important element of the electronic media.

Television people claimed that they were unfairly treated by government, which exercises control over the electronic media through the Federal Communications Commission. How did this come about—the control? And was it unfairly exercised? History has those answers, too. The record of electronic journalism is there for the public to examine, and it is part of the purpose of this book to examine it.

There were many other aspects of the media in the 1970s, from underground newspapers to public television. Did these figure in the question of the freedom of the media, and, if so, in what way? These questions need examination, too.

Then there are the questions of government operations, public policy, and the press. If the government works in secrecy and that secrecy is violated by the press, does this hurt the nation? The dispute over publication of the "Pentagon Papers" provided a look at this problem. Was freedom of the press threatened in the Pentagon Papers affair? Were there other issues beyond the freedom of the media to consider in this affair? And which issues, if there were others, were the most important?

Just how free is the American press? How free should it be? Should all the wraps be taken off every kind of information, as much of the press seems to wish? Should all journalists be completely unrestricted? Should the press and the electronic media be subsidized by government in any way, as is done in other countries, France, for example?

These are all questions within the general subject of the freedom of the media of information, or the news media. Past and current history can provide the facts. As to opinions, the authors have theirs, but readers are invited to make their own examination of the facts and come to their own conclusions about the state of the news media in America in the 1970s.

CHAPTER 1

From the Beginning: Freedom

The history of the American press basically is the history of the United States, for although printing came to the colonies shortly after the first settlers did (in 1638), and the first press was set up at Cambridge, Massachusetts, and became an adjunct of Harvard College, this was not newspapering as we know it today. There were no newspapers, or free printing, according to the laws of the colonies. The British lords and masters did not want these freedoms for the Crown Colonies. As Sir William Berkeley, who was governor of Virginia for thirty-four years, commented in 1671 when writing back to his native England:

I thank God, we have not free schools nor printing, and I hope we shall not have [them] these hundred years. For learning has brought disobedience and heresy and sects into the world; and printing has divulged them and libels against the government. God keep us from both.

Luckily, for the colonies and for the future of the country, Sir William's hopes were to prove vain.

English newspapers circulated in the colonies, and chief among them was the official London *Gazette*, which had been founded in 1665. But it was not until printing had existed in the colonies for over half a century that a newspaper was published by the Americans; up to this point printing was strictly a commercial venture, and nothing was printed that would cause any offense to the parent English government.

The first newspaper published in the American colonies had a short life. *Publick Occurrences both Foreign and Domestick* was first printed in Boston by Benjamin Harris on September 25, 1690. Alas, it had but one issue. The governor was offended because Harris had not asked for consent to publish; in addition, the government felt that the paper carried "sundry doubtful and uncertain reports." So *Publick Occurrences* was suppressed without ado.

It was fourteen years, then, before the first continuously published American newspaper appeared—the Boston *News-Letter*, founded by John Campbell on April 24, 1704. This weekly was published by the authority of the government, and the proprietor, eager to stay out of trouble, was extremely cautious. Much more famous, and rightly so, was the weekly Boston *Gazette*, started on December 21, 1719. Its first printer was James Franklin, whose apprentice was his thirteen-year-old brother Benjamin. The venture soon proved too tame for James Franklin, and he founded—without proper government authorization—the *New England Courant*, launched as an anti-smallpox-inoculation paper in August 1721. It appealed to a strong prejudice of the day against this medical treatment. By 1735 the growing city of Boston had a population of 20,000 and its choice of five newspapers serving various interests, most of them commercial.

In the twentieth century we often lament newspaper "mergers," but it is interesting to note that the first half of the eighteenth century marked the first consolidation of newspapers. In 1741 the Boston *Journal* publishers bought the old *Gazette* and merged the papers. Young Benjamin

Franklin had long before left that *Gazette* and moved to Philadelphia, where he bought the Pennsylvania *Gazette* in 1729.

We think of New York as first in most American cultural enterprises, but New York was the third colonial city to support a newspaper, when William Bradford launched the New York *Gazette* in November 1725. Newspapering in New York City gained fame over a court case concerning John Peter Zenger, whose name has become famous in the history of freedom of the press. Zenger had founded the New York *Weekly Journal* to support an antigovernment political position in the colony. He printed articles claiming that the freedoms and property of the people of New York were in actual danger because of a repressive government. His writings were so inflammatory that they were called "seditious libels" by officials.

The government council had Zenger arrested and put in jail, where he stayed for nine months. The authorities were embarrassed when Zenger refused to accept bail, but Zenger knew the values of publicity and martyrdom, and he edited his paper from jail until he came to trial on August 4, 1735.

Zenger's case had seemed hopeless; the New York governing authorities disbarred any local lawyers who attempted to defend the accused. But Andrew Hamilton, a famous lawyer of the time, came up from Pennsylvania to defend Zenger, and was so successful that the jury declared Zenger not guilty. The Zenger case was the first concerning the freedom of the press in America, and it established a broad avenue for future freedom.

During the Colonial period most American newspapers were edited and published by *printers,* not editors, and most news was foreign news. Few papers printed accounts of local affairs, nor did they publish many editorial comments. The device for most of the comments that did appear was the letter to the editor, usually addressed to a popular topic. Otherwise few papers dared to comment openly about the quarrels and relations of the colonists with the royal governor. It was only after the British Parliament passed the obnoxious Stamp Act that American newspapers began to be more concerned with political discussion.

The Stamp Act demanded that all printing be done on specially stamped, *taxed* paper. So great was public opposition to the act and so great the threat to the printers that the newspapers felt bound to report resistance to the act. By the time the act was actually to go into operation, the public outcry was so widespread that no one had the courage to actually distribute the stamped paper. Thus some newspapers published as usual, others suspended, and others changed their names and formats. Although the Stamp Act was soon repealed, it was followed by new taxes on goods, including tea and paper. Again the colonists were aroused, and they banded together to boycott goods from England—nonimportation, it was called.

Among the most actively anti-British newspapers was the *Gazette* of Boston. This paper printed the news and also published partisan articles by various literary contributors, among them many famous men in American history: Samuel Adams, John Adams, John Hancock. As tempo and tempers quickened, the patriot newspapers printed more and more antigovernment material. Some papers tried to print both sides, that of the patriots and that of the Tories, but because general public opinion was so aroused and anti-British, those papers were uniformly unsuccessful except in Tory territory. Tory publishers were hanged in effigy. Tory papers were forced to close. Of course, as the British troops began to take over Boston and other towns, the patriot papers were forced to suspend or move or even go underground. (One publisher actually buried his press and printing equipment.)

In the last years before the Revolution the newspapers lined up on the two sides. If nothing more, they were now a definite force, presenting biased, persuasive sentiment, either for or against the British. During the Revolution, the American newspapers did their best to report the military actions, although sometimes days and weeks after the events. There were no reporters or any systematic way of gathering news. Private letters and semiofficial and official messages provided the bulk of the information about the war. All newspaper publishers felt free to use anything they saw in other papers on war, politics, and even items of local interest.

The first so-called syndicated column made a brief appearance during this period. It was called the "Journal of Occurrence" and was edited by the Boston patriots. A number of newspapers in the colonies used the column as "news," but it also was definitely opinion and anti-British propaganda. Other editorial comments appeared in some papers, often as before via letters to the editor, with the writer using a pen name for self-protection. There was really no legal restraint on the press at this time; but there was restraint of a kind we do not know today: public opinion (in the form of mobs and threatened violence) censored many pro-Tory papers.

By the war's end, the anti-British newspapers had gained respectability and significant power. They had attracted much public attention, from their first bold opposition to the British at the time of the Stamp Act throughout their use during the Revolution as the patriots' propaganda weapon. Some readers believed implicitly everything the newspapers reported—a far cry from the American attitude toward journalism in the second half of the twentieth century.

After the Revolution printers were challenged as publishers by men who had discovered the value of newspapers as propaganda tools. Into the field now came "editors" who wanted to express a particular viewpoint. Most newspapers before and during the Revolution had been weeklies. With the growth of cities and commerce came the rise of dailies, and they flourished in the port cities of Philadelphia, New York, Baltimore, and Charleston. A partial reason for the success of the dailies was that news of the shipping and movement of vessels, which in the past had been bulletined daily at the local coffee houses, could now be incorporated into the newspapers.

At first the dailies were primarily mercantile newspapers, but, as political squabbling replaced revolutionary fervor, many newspapers became vehicles for political expression. Both types of papers flourished then, side by side.

The first concern of the new nation after the Revolution was the *type* of government it would have, and the Constitutional Convention was held to determine it. The new constitution that the convention developed caused much debate. The Federalists favored a strong central government; they wanted the proposed new constitution adopted. The anti-Federalists (later called Republicans and still later Democrats) fought against ratification of the proposed constitution. The heated opinions of the two forces were reflected in the newspapers. For example, Alexander Hamilton, James Madison, and John Jay defended the proposed constitution in a series of writings called *The Federalist Papers*. These were reprinted in Federalist newspapers throughout the country and were damned in anti-Federalist papers. Newspapers of both persuasions also aired and commented upon many other problems facing the new nation.

The first seat of the federal government was New York

City. Since there was no strong Federalist newspaper in New York, one was established, the *Gazette of the United States*, which supported President George Washington and the point of view of his administration. (There really were no political parties when Washington was chosen as the first President, but he basically stood for the Federalists, while those who had been anti-Constitution rallied around Thomas Jefferson, who was Secretary of State in Washington's cabinet.)

When the government moved to Philadelphia, the *Gazette* went along. Threatened by financial failure, the paper was subsidized by Alexander Hamilton, a Federalist party leader. The anti-Federalists, the Jefferson group, established another newspaper, the *National Gazette*, to express their point of view. The antigovernment paper, naturally, attacked and ridiculed the actions and policies of the government and its organ.

These rival papers were not at all restrained either in their comments or in their *personal* attacks on their political opponents. President Washington was almost constantly enraged at the contumely the opposition newspapers heaped upon him. Politically, Washington-baiting might be profitable; financially, however, the *National Gazette* was a failure. Its point of view was taken up by a new paper, the *Aurora*, published by a grandson of Benjamin Franklin, which, while it continued the scurrilous attacks on Washington, paid more attention to business.

Other politically outspoken newspapers existed in the larger Eastern cities like Philadelphia, and in some of the smaller cities there were also newspapers of importance. Newspapers sprang up farther west as new causes arose, such as the push for territorial status and later statehood. Wher ever papers existed they uniformly enjoyed freedom. An exception was Massachusetts where the state taxed the newspapers.

At first the majority of the states guaranteed freedom of the press in their constitutions, but when the federal Constitution was first drawn up, it had no such guarantees, an omission that caused much debate. Alexander Hamilton, for example, felt that there was no need for such written guarantees. He said: "What is the Liberty of the Press? Who can give it any definition which does not leave the utmost latitude for evasion?"

The question was resolved, however, when Congress adopted the first ten amendments, the Bill of Rights, at its first session. The first of these amendments is the basis for our press freedoms:

Congress shall make no law respecting an establishment of religion or prohibiting the free exercise thereof; or abridging the freedom of speech, or of the press; or the right of the people peaceably to assemble, and to petition the Government for a redress of grievances.

Since it was difficult to define freedom of the press, and its limitations, or nonlimitation, personal attacks for political reasons continued. The recourses were few: a man could physically beat up another or challenge him to a duel; libel suits could be filed. But generally speaking the American press was, as one judge said, "abominably gross and defamatory."

The first really important and effective attempt to curtail the freedom of the press was contained in the Alien and Sedition Acts of 1798. War with France was in the air, and the government decided on wartime measures, although hostilities had not occurred.

Three-quarters of the law concerned aliens, of whom there were many in the United States: the French who had come to America during the French Revolution, and many English and Irish refugees. The alien part of the acts affected only a few (but some prominent) Republican, antigovernment editors of newspapers. John D. Burk of the New York *Time Piece* was an Irishman whose position was already shaky since he was under indictment for libeling President Adams. Burk went into hiding rather than face possible deportation as an alien.

The sedition part of the acts was the most dangerous one as far as freedom of the press was concerned. This part stated that any person convicted of writing, printing, or uttering any "false, scandalous, and malicious" statement "against the government of the United States, or either house of the Congress, with intent to defame" or bring them into "contempt or disrepute" could be imprisoned for two years and fined $2,000. Thus the newspapers of Republican persuasion could no longer continue their attacks upon the government, but were to be gagged. A number of prominent newspaper editors suffered under this law.

There were also a great number of ridiculous cases, such as that of a man in Trenton who was fined $100 because he had said he wished President Adams had been hit in the britches with the wadding of the cannon which had been fired to salute him.

More serious, however, was the case of the *Aurora*, the leading antigovernment paper. Its editor was indicted, but died before trial. His successor refused to temper the paper's position and its attacks on President Adams, and he was the defendant in several suits.

Dr. Thomas Cooper, who emigrated from England to America in 1794, called President Adams incompetent, and for that, under the Sedition Act, he was fined $400 and sent to prison for six months. At his trial he had tried to secure Adams as a witness, intending to prove the "truth" of his statement, thus denying it was libel. But the court refused to issue a subpoena for Adams.

Other Republican newspapers were harassed when they continued to publish "libel against the government." There were more jail sentences and more fines. The act was definitely a government attempt to silence its newspaper critics. Fortunately, it was passed to last only the term of the then-current administration. The law expired when President Adams left office in 1801. Many claimed that sentiment against the acts helped to defeat Adams and elect Thomas Jefferson, the Republican leader, as President.

The first third of the nineteenth century brought increased numbers of newspapers, with no lessening of political vituperation in their pages. Presidents were attacked often, and bitterly. As usual there was the administration newspaper to defend the presidential works and the newspaper of the opposition in Washington to attack them. Editorials were the instruments for policy, but jibes, sneers, and innuendoes flowed over into other parts of the papers. There were many libel cases.

One of the most interesting of these cases (but hardly very important, except to the principal) was the suit against P. T. Barnum, the showman, early in the nineteenth century. Barnum was sued for libel repeatedly, and one might say impartially that he deserved to be sued for libel, since in his Danbury, Connecticut, newspaper he was very free with his comments about everything and everybody. After one of the trials, he was sentenced to sixty days in jail. He served his jail term, but during it continued to edit his paper, and the sympathy of the town was with him. When he was released from jail the people of Danbury greeted him with brass bands, cannon salutes, and laudatory orations.

Perhaps more effective in holding down abuse than libel cases was the duel. The classic case here was the duel in 1804 between Aaron Burr and Alexander Hamilton that resulted in Hamilton's death. The two men were leaders of rival political groups and bitter enemies. Each had his own newspaper with which to attack the other. The duel was prompted by remarks Hamilton had allegedly made in conversation— among them that Burr was "a dangerous man"; the remarks were printed in an Albany paper.

The principle that the duty of a reporter is to protect his news source was established at this time when several journalists refused to divulge their sources of information. In the House of Representatives in 1812 Nathaniel Rounsavell of the Alexandria *Herald* was jailed for refusing to tell his source for a story about secret proceedings in the House. He stood firm and won out.

The Washington newspapers were then the most strident. The most important of the Washington papers was the *National Intelligencer,* which had been started at the suggestion of Jefferson when he was running for President in 1800. It became the official organ of the federal government, and all other newspapers based their news of the government on the *Intelligencer*'s reports. Even after Jefferson left office, the paper continued for some years as the official organ of Presidents.

Andrew Jackson's friends established the *United States Telegraph* in Washington in 1826, after Jackson lost his bid for the Presidency to John Quincy Adams. When Jackson ran again the *Telegraph* was instrumental in his election, and it then became the official organ of the Jackson administration. A more important paper, however, was the Washington *Globe*, started in 1830, which was controlled by three men, Francis P. Blair of Kentucky, Amos Kendall, the chief editorial contributor, and John C. Rives. These men not only ran the *Globe* but were important members of President Jackson's so-called Kitchen Cabinet, the group of unofficial advisors who, it was said, had more power with Jackson than did his official cabinet.

The Washington newspapers were not the only vocal members of the press. Newspapers in New York, Boston, Philadelphia, Baltimore, and the deeper South were also outspoken in their political views. With the purchase of Louisiana and the migration to the western states and territories, the press followed and flourished almost everywhere, without restraint.

CHAPTER 2

The Independent Press

In the second half of the nineteenth century a drastic change in the course and importance of newspapers in the United States came with the appearance of what was called the "penny press." Until then newspapers generally had been sold on a yearly subscription basis, averaging 6 cents a copy. Now the papers would be sold on a daily basis, for a penny a copy.

These penny papers did not have a great intellectual impact, but their cheap price enabled moıe people to buy a newspaper. At the same time an increase in literacy created a larger reading audience. This audience was not made up of the kind of people who subscribed to the more politically conscious, more sophisticated press of the various parties or to the merchandising press. They were generally less-educated people. The penny press had to appeal to their interests and concerns, and it did.

For example, the first successful penny paper was the New York *Sun,* which appeared in 1833. It immediately began publishing in great detail the police court reports, which no paper had done before, and from there went on to print whatever it thought might titillate its readers.

The *Sun* perpetrated one of the greatest hoaxes in newspaper history. It printed a report that the distinguished astronomer, Sir John Herschel, had looked through a new telescope and discovered other planets. Then the newspaper reported that Sir John had also seen objects on the moon, and it went on to describe the moon's flora and fauna, dwelling particularly on strange creatures that inhabited that celestial body. The *Sun* obviously had a "scoop," and circulation soared. Soon other newspapers republished the articles. The *Sun* continued to hoax its gullible readers until an editor's confession exposed the story as a fraud.

In spite of this irresponsibility—or perhaps because of it—the *Sun* was financially successful. A spate of other penny dailies began to copy its style, among them the New York *Herald*, founded by James Gordon Bennett. The *Herald*, another flamboyant paper, attracted many readers—so many that its circulation did not suffer when it raised its price to two cents. There were penny papers in many other cities, and one of note was the Baltimore *Sun*. Unlike the mercantile and political papers, the penny papers' main publishing function was *not* the support of a political party.

Despite the rise of the penny press, political newspapers continued to retain an important position on the American newspaper scene. The *Evening Post* was the Democratic paper in New York. It had a most literate editor, William Cullen Bryant, who wholeheartedly supported the ruling Democratic party. James Watson Webb's *Courier and Enquirer* was New York's chief opposition—Whig—paper. But Horace Greeley became the most influential Whig editor. Greeley started the New York *Tribune* as a regular penny daily and later supplemented it with a *Tribune* weekly edition. By 1860 the *Tribune* had achieved the then fantastic circulation of 200,000. *The New York Times* was founded shortly after the *Tribune*, partly in reaction to the cheap sensationalism of much of the penny press. It adopted a high moral and literary tone and was, of course, politically active, too. It began as a Whig paper, then turned to the Free-Soilers, and then to the Republican party.

In the midnineteenth century the freedom of the press was never seriously questioned, even though the newspapers abused their freedom constantly with excesses of various kinds. Most threats to "freedom" came from individuals who disagreed with a paper's point of view, although in the 1830s a United States postmaster refused to deliver certain abolitionist (antislavery) newspapers. Still, government was not basically involved in the matter.

The chief threat to antislavery newspapers came from mobs that wrecked and destroyed their printing plants. The *Pennsylvania Freeman* in Philadelphia was sacked and burned in 1838; the *Free South* of Newport, Kentucky, was wrecked in 1859. But the most tragic result of trying to suppress the press was the murder of the Rev. Elijah P. Lovejoy, an ardent abolitionist, in Alton, Illinois, in 1837. Three times mobs destroyed his press, and in his fourth attempt to publish Lovejoy was shot and killed.

There was, of course, criticism of the press during this period. James Fenimore Cooper, the writer, felt so strongly that the press was an evil influence that he brought many private and criminal libel suits against the newspapers and won a surprising number of cases. After English author Charles Dickens visited the United States in 1842, he wrote:

While that press has its evil eye in every house, and its black hand in every appointment in the state, from a president to a postman, while, with ribald slander for its only stock in trade, it is the standard literature of an enormous class.

But the freedom of the American press continued practically unassailed.

During the Civil War censorship of the press was very sporadic, although the reporting and comment of the northern press were often anything but helpful to the Union war effort, and many northern newspapers did in fact print military information that could be construed as helping the southern forces. Even the War Department's order forbidding news of military or naval movements was generally ignored. There were infrequent punishments for infractions of the law. For example, a New York *Herald* correspondent was court-martialed and sentenced to six months hard labor for printing forbidden material.

During the war there were almost as many opinions about the conduct of the war as there were newspapers. Sometimes the Lincoln administration was forced to act as active censor when it felt opposition to the administration's war policies was too injurious to the Union. At one point, several New York newspapers, the *Journal of Commerce* and the *Daily News* among them, were accused of encouraging the rebels, and the New York postmaster was ordered not to accept those papers for mailing.

The Chicago *Times*, a sensational sheet, printed violent attacks on Lincoln, and it published any military news it chose to print—secret or not. It protected its right to do so by equipping its office with guns to thwart mob action. Finally, in 1864, General Burnside, who was military commander in Ohio, ordered the paper seized and suspended, and it was only by the intercession of President Lincoln that the paper renewed publication. After this incident a group of New York newspapermen, led by Horace Greeley, announced the principle that the press had every right to criticize civil and military acts of government but it should not be permitted to advocate outright treason or rebellion. Considering the venality of much of the press in the Civil War, the Lincoln administration was really very restrained in dealing with the northern press.

The greatest censorship in the North came from the public: angry mobs wrecked and destroyed those newspapers with which they disagreed. The violence of American society was, then, the chief danger to press freedom.

In the South it was a different matter. Many southern papers were destroyed, suppressed, or censored by the military, especially during federal occupation of such cities as Memphis, Vicksburg, and New Orleans. They were, of course, treated as "enemy" newspapers. When Reconstruction came, there was not much improvement in the freedom of the southern papers, for the carpetbaggers in control forced the opposition papers into silence.

Whether from exhaustion or moral growth, newspapers in the post-Civil War period generally adopted a more responsible attitude toward their function. News reporting assumed greater importance, replacing the political polemic, and a number of newspapers, especially those of Democratic leanings, mounted serious and effective campaigns against the official corruption that characterized the administration of President Ulysses S. Grant. Such weeklies as *Leslies' Weekly*, *Harper's Weekly*, and the *Nation*, whose contributors were distinguished men of letters, also exerted considerable influence.

The New York Times and *Harper's Weekly* carried out a vigorous campaign against Boss William Tweed and Tammany Hall in New York City. Thomas Nast, cartoonist for *Harper's Weekly*, proved the impact of the editorial cartoon by successfully stirring up a group of concerned citizens to prosecute the Tweed Ring. This ring had great political power and was extremely corrupt, mulcting huge sums of money from the public.

Established newspapers increased their circulations in the years following the Civil War (the circulation of the Boston *Herald*, for example, reached 100,000), and the number of papers skyrocketed. By 1870 the United States had three times as many newspapers as did the United Kingdom and more than a third of all the newspapers in the world. By 1880, the U.S. had about 7,000 newspapers, or double the 1870 figure, and by 1890 there were over 12,000. This was a period of independent journalism, not journalism tied to the apron strings of politics.

Such independent newspapers were founded and grew splendidly in the South and the West. From St. Louis came Joseph Pulitzer, who was to make a tremendous mark on New York journalism with the *World*. In a way, the *World* illustrated the essential ambivalence that continues to dog American newspapers: Pulitzer made news coverage the backbone of the paper, and he supported an editorial page of high caliber that conducted effective crusades. Yet the *World* indulged in sensationalism and stunts of dubious value to increase circulation. (One of the most famous *World* reporters was "Nellie Bly," among whose adventures was an around-the-world trip from New York to better the record of Phileas Fogg of Jules Verne's fictitious *Around the World in 80 Days*. Nellie used sampans and burros and other modes of transportation, and all of this was detailed in the *World* day after day.)

The *World*'s sensationalism was condemned but copied by many competitors, foremost among them William Randolph Hearst's *Journal*. The competition between these two papers centered on their Sunday papers, which featured color comic strips. Thus was born the phrase "yellow journalism"—after the *Journal*'s comic-strip character, the "Yellow Kid." It came to symbolize a type of razzle-dazzle newspapering.

But Hearst and Pulitzer did not fight their circulation battles merely with comic strips. Both the *Journal* and the *World* waged their own war as they whipped the reading public into a frenzy to launch the U.S. into a war with Spain in 1896. They printed sensational stories of Spanish atrocities against the Cuban people, and after the sinking of the U.S. battleship *Maine* in Havana harbor, they continued their circulation war by publishing misrepresentation of facts, some inventions, and reckless headlines. During the Spanish-American War that followed, censorship by the military was lenient, and American journalists were almost completely free in action and reporting.

After the Spanish-American War yellow journalism, with its scare headlines, frauds, misleading information, increased use of sensational pictures, and comics, spread rapidly over the country and reached its zenith around 1900—still without curbs on its abuse of its freedom.

In the last years of the nineteenth century and early years of the twentieth, there first appeared an ill that would thereafter beset the newspapers: the establishment of newspaper chains, usually through the consolidation of ownership. With the coming of chain newspapers, public confidence in newspapers tended to diminish. The papers were as free as ever, in spite of the concentration of economic and editorial power that chain newspapering represents. But chain newspapers usually followed a unified editorial policy on national and international issues. This raised eyebrows.

One of the first successful chain newspaper owners was

E. W. Scripps. In one sense Scripps went against his times, which called for newspapers to be "big business." Population in the United States had doubled, and the average circulation of newspapers had also doubled. With all the mechanical inventions, printing and publishing were often outside the ability of the individual entrepreneur.

Scripps claimed that although it might take millions of dollars to start a newspaper in New York City, elsewhere papers could be started with little more than a basement, a few machines, and a shoestring amount of cash. Following this philosophy of founding new papers instead of buying old ones, E. W. Scripps by the beginning of World War I owned interests in thirty-four newspapers in fifteen states. His papers prospered in part because they crusaded for causes, a technique used widely by many papers of the period. The New York papers, the sensational Denver *Post* of Bonfils and Tammen, the St. Louis *Post-Dispatch,* the Philadephia *North American,* all crusaded. Projects ranged from campaigns against local bossism to attacks on ice and coal monopolies to good works—raising money for flood and earthquake victims—to campaigns for better schools and roads. It was also a time of muckraking, which reached its peak on such magazines as *Colliers'* and *McClure's* with, for example, Samuel Hopkins Adams's attack on the patent medicine business and Ida Tarbell's account of Standard Oil policies and practices.

Here again, papers were free to be yellow or politically radical, free to champion, free to denounce, free to amuse, educate, or report. The only papers to suffer any restraint were those considered "communistic" and "anarchistic," after an amendment to the federal code was passed in 1911 making it a crime to publish "matters of a character tending to incite arson, murder, or assassination." The Postmaster General could refuse to let such matter into the mails.

The only effort of the government to prosecute newspaper publishers for criminal libel occurred in a case in 1910 when President Theodore Roosevelt sought action against the Indianapolis *News* and the New York *World* after these newspapers charged the U.S. Attorney General and others with making personal profits from the Panama Canal purchase. But in this case federal judges up to the Supreme Court upheld the right of newspapers to do their duty in investigating public matters and refused to uphold the Roosevelt administration's complaint.

One might say that Teddy Roosevelt was the first President of modern times to try to suppress the freedom of the press—and he failed because the institution of freedom was so well established in American society that, irresponsible as the press might be, the public would not condone its suppression.

During World War I correspondents were at first censored by various European military officials. After the U.S. entered the war, various proclamations were issued by President Woodrow Wilson controlling press freedom in the national interest as the administration saw it. First of all, any publishers who printed information or views that would give "aid and comfort to the enemy" were liable to prosecution for treason. Then came the Espionage Act of June 15, 1917, which provided for fines and even imprisonment of anyone who "shall wilfully cause or attempt to cause . . . disloyalty." Or anyone who "shall wilfully obstruct recruitment." Any journal or paper that contained such material could not be mailed.

Later, in October 1917, came the Trading with the Enemy

Act, which brought outright censorship of all messages sent abroad and forced newspapers containing articles in a foreign language to file sworn translations with local postmasters.

The Sedition Act of May 1918 provided for fines and imprisonment for the writing or publication of "any disloyal, profane, scurrilous or abusive language about the form of government of the United States," and any language which would bring the United States or American society into "contempt, scorn, contumely, or disrepute." The Postmaster General's word was supreme, and he held power over the mailing privileges.

These were tough laws, but it was an equally tough war. Some German-Americans must obviously have felt that their basic freedoms were impinged or denied. And so they were. In wartime, even in democracies and democratic Republics, there is no absolute freedom.

During World War I most of the newspapers in the United States adhered to either the stated or the voluntary censorship rules. The newspapers that got into trouble were generally those of the German-American and Socialist press, and some of the Hearst newspapers, which were distinctly opposed to Great Britain and France.

In this period more and more newspapers consolidated, or formed chains. Morning and afternoon newspapers were often owned by the same publisher. Not only did Scripps continue to gather in papers, but so did Frank Munsey, who felt that small operations lost money and that consolidation was the answer. Cities that had had competing newspapers now found themselves with one newspaper voice. William Randolph Hearst merged great dailies, until he had built up a veritable newspaper empire. Smaller operators formed smaller groups within smaller areas—the regional chain became common. There were constant changes, including the emergence of the tabloid newspaper (a paper half the size of the ordinary one), which soon obtained a reputation for sensationalism. The tabloids covered murders, trials, and scandals with immense vigor and execrable taste, before they became somewhat tempered by time.

The newspapers of the 1920s and 1930s on up until the Second World War continued to cover the news as they saw it. The news coverage became more complete, including much more emphasis on foreign news and more interpretation through the wider use of columnists. Wire services, such as the Associated Press and United Press and International News Service (the latter two later merging as the United Press International, or UPI) served smaller papers that did not have wide-ranging correspondents of their own.

In the thirties several cases called attention to the freedom of the press and threats against it. One occurred in 1930-31 in the "Gag Law" of Minnesota. This law stated that "malicious, scandalous, and defamatory" newspapers and periodicals could be suppressed by injunction as public nuisances. The Minneapolis *Saturday Press* published a series of articles speaking out against vice and gambling conditions. The state sought an injunction to stop the paper. The U.S. Supreme Court said that libel laws protect against the wrongs that appear in publications, but injunction cannot be used to suppress the press—it would be a violation of the Bill of Rights.

World War II was the most thoroughly covered war in history; hundreds of correspondents swarmed over the battlefields and outposts of Europe and the Pacific, detailing for the American public exactly what was taking place. There were eyewitness reports, military reports, color, drama, news—it was all there. And since it was war, there was, of course, censorship.

Shortly after Pearl Harbor, in December 1941, the U.S. Office of Censorship was established by the powers granted President Roosevelt under the first War Powers Act. Through this body, all communications entering or leaving the United States, by mail, cable, or radio, were censored—changed, passed, or suppressed—but only to eliminate information that might help the enemies of the United States. In addition to this legal body there was also established a "Code of Wartime Practices for the American Press," a system of voluntary censorship by the editors and publishers themselves. The problems, when they occurred, involved the question of what constituted aid and comfort to the enemy. It was possible that even a weather report could fall in that category —so all-pervasive had war become on twentieth-century life. Yet both these programs were generally considered successful.

Labor costs rose sharply after the war, and as a consequence, so did newspaper consolidations. While some chains, such as the Newhouse chain, permitted local editorial autonomy, others reflected more the views of the consolidator. Newspapers *were* big business, but now, in addition to the threat to survival posed by their labor costs, newspapers would also be threatened by television.

Throughout those years immediately following World War II press freedom was rarely assaulted or questioned. Some complaints were heard, though, during the Korean War in the early fifties: the military commanders railed against the correspondents and the latter resented General Douglas MacArthur's stringent censorship.

Following World War II and the Korean War, and continuing into the 1970s, the question of classified documents and records maintained by the government became more and more controversial. The press quite properly regarded such blanket secret classification as an unwarranted restriction of the right to report, and the government quite properly considered such classification the protection of military and political security. The difference was a matter of degree. Sometimes the press revealed matters that were hurtful to American policies. Sometimes the government representatives tried to use—and did use—secrecy as a means of suppressing exposure and debate of unpleasant subjects, inefficiencies, skulduggery, and policies that many Americans did not approve.

The issue of press freedom grew as the U.S. government embarked on the adventure of a war in Southeast Asia that became more unpopular year by year, from the early 1960s onward.

CHAPTER 3

The Daily Newspaper and Freedom

After three decades of upheaval, in the 1970s the American daily newspaper appeared to have achieved a working stability as an institution. If this occurred at the expense of the weaker papers, which largely died out, that is the inexorable law of competitive economics.

The most recent major change as of this writing was the elimination of the Washington *Daily News* from the scene of the nation's capital, making Washington a two-newspaper city like so many other large metropolitan centers today. In the case of the Washington *Daily News* there was a historic difference—for once the chain did not swallow the independent, but the independent swallowed the chain newspaper. The *Daily News* was part of the Scripps-Howard chain while the *Evening Star*, which bought it out, is a big independent. But to say that the ever-present trend toward the concentration of the economic power of the media was reversed would be to oversimplify. The Washington *Evening Star* complex consisted of television and radio properties in Washington and several other southern cities. The fact was that there simply was not enough advertising and circulation revenue to go around—in 1972 the *Star* had been losing money for two years, the *Daily News* for five years. The *Star* was in a stronger position and won out, and almost certainly would survive.

Loss of advertising and circulation revenue represents the primary economic threat to the well-being and thus the freedom of the newspaper press in America. What had happened to the press in the passing century was that it had ceased to be the primary purveyor of information—at least in the national field and in the field of immediate events.

Nor had it been able to perpetuate the tradition of the giant editors. Horace Greeley, Charles Dana, Henry J. Raymond—these were the editorial names to conjure with in the 1870s. William Randolph Hearst, Joseph Pulitzer, these were the names of the following thirty years, and they were matched in the far West by editors like M. H. DeYoung of San Francisco and Harvey W. Scott of Portland. These people were known far beyond the range of their newspaper interests. They were civic leaders, and they were praised and damned in the manner of public figures everywhere.

In the decades to follow came other powerful names: the Cowles brothers, Eugene Pulliam, John S. Knight. Yet these people never had the public power of their predecessors, although the economic power they wielded was far more pervasive. And along with these names came others: Silliman Evans, Richard J. Finnegan, Palmer Hoyt; these men were managers, their claim to fame rested on their professionalism and their involvement in public affairs. Erwin Canham, the editor of the *Christian Science Monitor*, and one of the most respected of American editors, was also known almost as well as a commentator for radio and television. For increasingly the editors were forced to share the old seats of respect and power with the new electronic journalism, and this changed the whole status of the newspaper everywhere.

In the past, the freedom of the press banner had been unfurled without embarrassment by such disparate characters as F. G. Bonfils of the Denver *Post* and William Allen White of the Emporia *Gazette* (two editors have never been more dissimilar in conduct and aims). It could readily cover both—the flamboyant front-page attacks without benefit of any warning of editorialization that were the mark of Bonfils; the causism of White, who became a symbol of respectability in journalism. The story of the *Post* was that F. G. had two lists: a list of people whose names could not appear in the *Post* unless something foul could be said about them and a list of people whose names could not appear *at all*. But Bonfils and his partner Harry Tammen were free to cover the news as they saw fit and to throw mud and bouquets as they chose. If people did not like it, they could read the *Rocky Mountain News* or the *Express* or the *Times*.

There, of course, was the great leavener—competition. In a way it served to control the antics of the press: a newspaper that fell completely out of favor would collapse—so the public in the final analysis maintained the control of the press. What happened to this old personal journalism, and the relationship of its decline to the press and its problems of maintenance of freedom are indicated in the development of newspapers in the years around and after World War II.

Few newspapers have been founded—and even fewer have succeeded—in the period since 1940. Ventures in liberal journalism, in particular, have generally been short-lived. A prime example was *P.M.* founded in New York by Marshall Field, the department-store heir. *P.M.* was a "rootin', tootin'" advocate of liberalism, as close to a "journal of opinion" as American newspapering has produced in the twentieth century. It just did not find an adequate market to support advertising, even in liberal New York City. Nor did its successor, the New York *Star*. Political journalism, of the type so common in the middle of the nineteenth century, simply would not pay off in the twentieth.

Another of Marshall Field's ventures did pay off, in Chicago. Field founded the Chicago *Sun,* a more traditional newspaper. By itself the *Sun* never really made it, but its ownership gave the Field interests a foothold in Chicago journalism. Then Field bought the Chicago *Times,* a very old newspaper that was in economic difficulties, too. He put the two together and came out with a lively round-the-clock-newspaper, the *Sun-Times,* which did manage to survive.

Another chapter in the continuing story of newspapering economics concerns what happened in Chicago a few years later. The *Sun-Times* bought up the Chicago *Daily News* from the Knight interests, while about the same time the Chicago *Tribune* bought up the *Herald-American* from the Hearst interests. The transactions were purely a matter of economics. There were no other reasons for the changes in ownership. Now, though, Chicago is a two-ownership town, even if the respective newspapers have kept something of their old identity.

Economics must be reckoned with, of course. But an unhappy by-product of economic survival through mergers is that the cause of freedom of the press, in the sense of the old spirit of diversity and competition, obviously has suffered a good deal. The melding, the homogenization of the press that goes on in a dozen ways, has, over the years, diminished the spectrum of ideas and presentations by the press, and newspapers have consequently lost many of the interesting aspects that formerly held the interest of the American people.

P.M. is a prime example of the obverse; so is the old Chicago *Tribune* before it was desanitized following the death of Colonel Robert McCormick. Whatever else one might say about *P.M.* and the *Tribune,* at least they were interesting. They provided topics of conversation—themselves—for the people, and in so doing they struck a blow for the whole, and for freedom. Colonel McCormick, for all his faults, was unmuzzleable, and all the world knew it.

Colonel McCormick apparently did not believe, however, that free expression and access to information were everyone's right. He was party to one of the baldest attempts by a private monopoly group to stifle press freedom in the United States. It happened in 1942, and besides McCormick and the *Tribune*, it involved the Chicago *Sun* and the Associated Press.

The Associated Press had been formed as a cooperative news agency back in the nineteenth century by various newspapers that wanted to be able to pool their regional news. As the country grew, the Associated Press became ever more important to national and world news coverage. There were quarrels about AP membership, and some newspapers were restricted from membership and thus were unable to get the services of the AP. In 1906 the Hearst people founded the International News Service, and in 1907 E. W. Scripps organized the United Press Associations. Both these news service organizations flourished for a number of years.

When Marshall Field started the *Sun*, he wanted the AP service. It was denied him under a restrictive by-law that gave an established newspaper—in this case McCormick's *Tribune*—a veto power over use of the AP service by a rival newspaper in the same city. The Roosevelt administration filed an antitrust suit against the AP, and the matter went through the courts. Justice Hugo Black wrote the Supreme Court's majority opinion (5-3) and said that freedom of the press did not sanction repression of the press by private interests. The First Amendment, said the court, did not protect combinations in restraint of trade, and the AP was forced to give the *Sun* its service.

So it can be seen that the factors that militate for repression of the press may lie within the press itself as well as without.

One of the delicate factors involving press freedom in the 1970s was the newspapers' internal financial picture. Because of the increase in newspaper circulation over the years and the centralization of economic power in the hands of fewer newspapers in various communities, the newspaper was still an enormously successful financial investment.

Get away from the big city for a moment and consider the situation of the medium-sized American daily newspaper. In recent years these newspapers have tended to be afternoon papers, published six days a week. *Editor and Publisher*, the trade journal of the newspaper business, analyzes the operating picture of various brackets of newspapers. Here are some of its findings for medium-sized newspapers in 1971:

> They had more revenue than in the past—5 per cent more than in 1970.
>
> Their expenses were higher—9 per cent more than in 1970.
>
> Their circulation revenue was increasing.
>
> Their columns of reading matter (as opposed to advertising) were decreasing—42,700 columns in 1970; 40,100 columns in 1971.
>
> Their profit before taxes was almost 30 per cent of sales.

A newspaper is a business, and the dichotomy of the newspaper as business and "public institution" must always be considered in relation to the freedom of the press. This dichotomy can be embarrassing: in 1972 Congress considered an ill-advised bill that would exempt the press from certain of the federal price controls, on the basis that this exemption would further the freedom of the press. Many responsible newspaper people objected. They were right to do so, because the newspaper does wear two hats. It is a business as well as a public institution, and its business aspect is apparent—sometimes painfully so—in the second half of the twentieth century.

In the best of all possible worlds the newspaper editor would divorce his policies entirely from economics. Practically, this does not happen: no newspaper can survive unless it first survives as a business, and in recent years the tendency has been for the newspaper to fall under business management more and under editorial management less.

As a result, in many cities, solid reporting has given way to "going through the motions," or to the new journalism that holds that it is neither important nor possible to attain objectivity. The editor has given way to the by-liner as a figure of importance in the newspaper, and the "Star System"—an unfortunate inheritance from television—has been allowed to develop. The syndicated columnist, who may achieve his fame by his appearances on television, has become the principal thinker for thousands of newspapers, particularly on national and international matters.

Over the whole operation stands the business manager, ready to cut costs to the marrow if necessary. On the medium-size daily, costs have been cut by reducing the percentage of payroll to other costs. This means either fewer people, usually on the editorial side, or no increase in editorial expenses, even when advertising revenues and the size of the paper have increased.

These situations are not easy for the newspaper. The publisher operates under tight restraints, some of which make life very difficult for the people who cover the news. The craftsmen—the printers, the stereotypers, and the pressmen in particular—have very strong, well-entrenched union organizations. Their concern by and large is purely job security and job-oriented. But once in a while the craft unions get involved in political matters that concern the freedom of the press. For example, one spring day in 1972 the press run of *The New York Times* was delayed for an hour because the pressmen refused to run off the paper. Their reason? They objected to a full-page advertisement in the paper that attacked President Richard Nixon on a public issue. The issue is unimportant; the fact that the pressmen chose to make editorial judgment was all-important, and it represents a very definite threat to the freedom of the press.

Similarly, a union action by the American Newspaper Guild in July 1972 created another spectre to haunt American newspapers: The Guild's national office announced the support of Democratic candidate George McGovern for the Presidency. Guild units at the Washington *Post, The New York Times*, and many other important and influential dailies protested. The action compromised the integrity of every political reporter who belonged to the American Newspaper Guild. That the action could be taken indicates the difficulty of the newspaperman who belongs to a union organization. But more important, and destructive, is the public reaction such a move was bound to create. McGovern supporters might be very pleased to have the Guild's support this time, but some thoughtful persons might also consider where the support might go "next time." But all newspaper readers would, after the Guild's declaration, have to consider whether the reporter covering the political campaign was writing a biased report and whether the subeditors of the newspaper were editing the report to suit their own convictions. Thus the Guild's action enlarged the credibility gap between the press and its readers and added another threat to the freedom of the press as an institution.

The credibility gap of newspapers has always existed, it was no phenomenon of the 1970s. Democrats believed Horace Greeley's New York *Tribune* no more than Republicans believed what they read in Dana's New York *Sun*. In Denver, Bonfils and Tammen's praise of a public official might lead the public to suspect that Bon and Tam had him in their pocket. In Portland, Oregon (in the days after Harvey Scott) the *Oregonian* was so right wing and so hated by many people that Rufus K. Holman won the governorship by campaigning against the *Oregonian* and all it stood for.

New Deal Democrats were not inclined to accept anything Colonel McCormick's Chicago *Tribune* had to state, editorially or in the news columns, about the progress of the Roosevelt administration. The same held true to a lesser extent of other newspapers. In those days, the bias was exerted by the editors and owners. The subtle difference in the 1970s was the diminution of influence of these movers and shakers, and the increase in influence of the business managers. But there was also a change in the newspapermen themselves. In the days of Franklin Roosevelt, the tradition of *The Front Page,* that is, of the hard-drinking, hard-working, underpaid newspaperman, was still fairly representative of the newspaper field. In the 1970s the newspaper reporter was much more likely to be a man or woman with advanced college degrees and a very high opinion of self, which may bring on spates of messianic zeal. There was nothing new in this development, except the frequency in which these exhalations found their way into the news pages of the newspaper.

In the 1940s and in the 1950s a reporter covering a story, particularly one with emotional, economic, or political significance, could easily become rapt in his subject and vent his opinions. But in those days, such a story would likely find its way onto the editor's spike. Or the writer would be directed with a firm finger to take his story to the Editorial Page Department, where he might try to persuade the editor either to accept his position or to print his article as a column of opinion.

Along with the banker and the lawyer and the doctor, the newspaper editor was once regarded as a substantial citizen in America and was expected to take a position of leadership in community affairs. If this picture is rosier than the facts of history warrant, still it was the way many good editors regarded themselves, and they attempted to live up to a high concept of community. Especially, they controlled their own voice, the voice of the newspaper. In the 1970s, the old responsible regard for community is rarely apparent among newspaper editors, and newspapers speak with so many voices that some readers are not inclined to pay much attention to them at all.

The fault is not entirely the newspaper proprietor's, though. For in many cases, the old editor-proprietor is no longer living, and the paper is in the hands of heirs, who are far more interested in the financial figures than in the community's problems. This was the case of both the Portland *Oregonian* and the *Oregon Daily Journal* in recent years— and is why they are now owned by the Newhouse chain, which has put Portland totally in the hands of outside owners as far as the newspapers are concerned.

In two other cases—the Milwaukee *Journal* and, as of 1972, the Denver *Post* following the death of Helen Bonfils, daughter of one of the founders—the newspapers passed into even more amorphous hands: those of the trust, which in the final analysis means the estate lawyers. No really strong editorial figure is likely to emerge from either situation.

Sometimes a newspaper falters when put in "committee" hands, as was the case of the Cleveland *Plain Dealer* after it was willed to the employees in trust. The *Plain Dealer* was also eventually sold to Newhouse.

More fundamental than the failure of the heirs, however, is the continuing amalgamation of newspapers into large or small chains. If there was any one basic truth about the newspaper business in the 1970s, it was that the multiple owners were taking over. The chains are very powerful. They include Newhouse, Knight, Hearst, Scripps-Howard, Gannett, Ridder, as well as many smaller chains that may own dozens of newspapers. What few people realized in the 1970s was that such newspapers as the Washington *Post* and *The New York Times* are both chain operations.

Like most corporate mergers, newspaper amalgamations are arranged for economic reasons and can be justified as good business practice. The growing prevalence of the mergers is evidence, though, that the newspaper business is becoming steadily more business and less newspaper—which poses a grave internal danger to the newspapers' freedom. The following few facts about the economics of newspapering during the decade of the 1960s should be a real cause for anxiety regarding press freedom:

> Chains bought an average of 40 independent newspapers each year during the 1960s.
>
> Half the nation's daily newspapers are now owned by chains.
>
> Most of the biggest daily newspapers are now owned by chains.
>
> Of a total of 1,600 cities, only 40 cities have more than one economically independent daily newspaper.

The threat to freedom in this change to the chain system of operation is no less great because it is insidious. Most of the chain operators pride themselves on the business concept with which they approach the newspaper business. The Newhouse chain, for example, claimed that its papers were under local editorial control. True, but in the election of 1968 one Newhouse editor refused to support any candidate for the Presidency "because it was too controversial." Thus a once-great newspaper failed in one of its primary duties to its readership, not only because the editor lacked gumption, but perhaps even more importantly because he appeared not even to know that it is the responsibility of the editor to take a definite editorial stance. The Newhouse management could never fault an editor for not getting in trouble, although trouble is where newspaper editors of the past flourished.

Equally important to the decline of the entrepreneur-editor in newspapering was the rise of the electronic media. Television, in particular, was making pretenses of "covering the news," and in questions of immediacy it could overpower the printed press. As radio had killed the newspaper "extra," so television killed another special: the big picture section or picture story; television could do it so much better. Also, television documentaries cut deeply into the "think" sections of newspapers, as far as readership was concerned.

In addition to disturbing the newspapers' readership pattern, television has taken the newspapers' advertising revenue. Yet by the 1970s the newspapers still had not learned to live with television, and by and large were functioning as they had been for at least thirty years. Instead of playing on the weaknesses and innate sensationalism of television news coverage and taking a more thoughtful, objective approach, many newspapers seemed to be trying to imitate some of the worst features of television reporting.

In line with this tendency, one of the greatest problems facing the American press in the 1970s was the so-called new journalism. The growing insistence of "newsmen" that they be allowed to express their personality in their writing was a pressure that threatened to overwhelm the editorial stance of many newspapers.

In the spring of 1972 the "new journalism" came into focus for the first time when its adherents staged (and the word is appropriate) the first A. J. Liebling Counter-Convention in New York.

All the names of new journalism were there: Gloria Steinem, Tom Wolfe, Gay Talese, Abbie Hoffman, and so on. Gore Vidal, the novelist, made the claim that "the only publications worth reading are the *New York Review of Books* and *Screw* magazine [one of the underground press publications]."

"I wanted more pay, a longer time to work on my stories, respect for my copy and better editors," said David Halberstam, once a reporter for *The New York Times*, when talking about why he left daily newspaper work.

The convention was an exercise in personal publicity for a handful of people and of virtually no use to anyone else. As Sally Quinn of the Washington *Post*, who covered the convention, put it: "But what many at the convention may have lost sight of is what A. J. Liebling once said: 'There is a healthy American newspaper tradition of not taking yourself seriously. It is the story you must take that way.' "

That was the problem of the new journalists—they were so self-conscious that they could not divert attention from themselves to the facts. Indeed, in the new journalism, the facts tended to meld into one another, obscured by the purpose of the writer, which was to project his personality and his ideas.

While the new journalists were meeting, the publishers across town were concerning themselves with this incipient rebellion in the newsroom and discussing "democracy" in news coverage. An old-time city editor would have rolled in his grave at the concept, let alone the words. The publisher of the Huntington (Indiana) *Herald* said, "It's the most nit-wit idea I've ever heard of in my life. I'm responsible for what's in my paper and I'm not going to delegate it to a democracy. We get off the track when we bring in all these freaks and weirdos."

This was the kind of problem that faced the editors and publishers of the 1970s. How they solved it might well determine whether American readers would continue to regard the newspapers with respect.

There was no question in the 1970s that the credibility gap was very wide. An excellent example of it was given by Professor Russel B. Nye of Michigan State University—where he was a professor of English, not of journalism. Professor Nye admitted freely that he had never trusted newspapers much, and perhaps that was because he grew up on the Chicago *Tribune*, in the heyday of Colonel McCormick. Prompted by this distrust and by curiosity on a subject that interested him, Professor Nye made a little check of his own on his subject over a period of time and wrote about it in *The Progressive*.

The subject was the number of draft resisters who had fled to Canada rather than join the United States Armed Forces. Martin Nolan of the Boston *Globe* had put the figure at 50,000, and he was quoting an article by James Reston, Jr., in the *New Republic*. In 1968 a writer for the *Progressive* said there were 10,000. *The New York Times* said 4,000. A Toronto antidraft group said 10,000. In 1969 a Toronto draft-resisters' group said 60,000 and in 1970 gave 60,000 as its "outside" figure. In 1970 the estimates varied from 6,000 to 60,000. In 1971 they went up as high as 70,000, depending upon whom one quoted. In 1972 they hit 100,000. In all this time, with all these variations, no newspaperman seemed to find it worthwhile to discover the facts, even though they were as easy to get as any facts not handed a reporter on a silver platter. Dr. Nye, who made such fact-getting something of a hobby, said this:

Most striking in the stories was the almost complete lack of plain legwork. I found no journalist who had consulted easily obtainable Canadian immigration figures, and with one or two exceptions, none who had researched the realities of the Canadian immigration laws. . . . Canadian embassy and consular sources that have no axe to grind will, if asked, estimate about 10,000 American draft evaders in Canada . . . but nobody asks them.

This was true, although at the time, in the spring of 1972, the question of amnesty for draft evaders was very much in the public mind and even came before Congress when hearings were held on the subject on Capitol Hill.

Dr. Nye's reaction to his own study was: "As for me, I trust the press no more than before."

And therein is a serious threat to freedom of the press in America, because when the majority of citizens come to the conclusion that the press, uniformly, is not to be trusted, then they will have no objection to muzzling that press. Indeed, they will tend to look with favor on the muzzling.

Another threat to press freedom on the internal scene came from the growing demands of militant minority pressure groups. It began with the failure of the newspapers, reflecting the total American society, to hire nonwhites as editorial workers. Even in recent years the situation was appalling; figures of the American Society of Newspaper Editors showed that in 1972 three quarters of 1 per cent of newspapermen were black, Chicano, Oriental, or Indian. In a newspaper work force of 40,000 that meant only 300 nonwhite members. This situation is a result of the American educational process, the discrimination against minorities over so many years—in short, the whole American social process.

American editors were trying: in 1971 William Block, publisher of the Pittsburgh *Post-Gazette*, let it be known that he was looking seriously for several competent black reporters. But few were to be had—and if the black activists had their way there might be even fewer. For one of the problems of the 1970s was the polarization of peoples: the black activists could be said to be represented by Tony Brown, dean of the school of communications of Howard University, the most prominent black university in the land. He had suggested that black journalists must be activist writers, involved in the promotion of the interests of the blacks.

The dilemma was indicated in the spring of 1972 when the Congressional Black Caucus (the blacks in the United States Congress) called hearings to explore the problems of black publicity. Lu Palmer, a columnist with the Chicago *Daily News,* testified that there were only eleven black reporters on the four big Chicago newspapers—noting that these newspapers were "white owned." Thirty-three per cent of Chicago's population is black.

Representative Shirley Chisholm from New York noted that the Washington *Star* had but 9 reporters who were black, among an editorial force of 185, in a city that was 71 per cent black. She also said that in New York, which was 21 per cent black, the *Times* had 20 minority reporters of 557 editorial workers. The San Francisco *Chronicle* (San Francisco has a 28.5 per cent minority population) had only 12 members of the minority groups working on its editorial staff that totaled 223 employees. She had checked eighteen Washington newspaper bureaus that together employed 73 reporters, but not one of the bureaus employed a black reporter.

Unwittingly, perhaps, the blacks seemed to be working in the spring of 1972 to make the situation worse rather than better. Some, like Lu Palmer, suggested that blacks in the general media world behave like ordinary citizens, not failing to criticize other blacks when their actions fell afoul of public policy. But most chose a narrower position: help the blacks, and "to hell" with the general public.

This position was strengthened in the eyes of the public (and in the eyes of newspaper publishers) when seven black reporters of the Washington *Post* filed an unfair practices complaint with the U.S. Equal Employment Opportunity Commission.

Thirty-seven of the 397 *Post* news employees were black, representing 10 per cent of the force. The blacks on the paper wanted better jobs, more black hiring, and a quota system. They pointed out again that Washington was more than 70 per cent black. What they did not point out was that the zone of circulation of Washington newspapers was more than 70 per cent white. The disparity in figures represented the movement of whites from the city proper to the suburbs —where they continued to read Washington newspapers and interest themselves in Washington affairs.

Post management was shocked at being singled out in this fashion. But for the most part these reporters and other editorial workers were black activists, or at least people vitally interested in their racial problems. Who could blame them? One does not expect philosophy from a man in a burning building; under the circumstances in which the blacks found themselves, it was remarkable in 1972 that there was as little trouble as there was.

As mentioned, William Block represented the publishers of goodwill; in 1971 he was sincerely trying to find blacks who could do the work. A reporter sent out to do a job carried with him the prestige and even the financial well-being of the paper. An untruthful or erroneous report could cause an expensive libel suit. It was obvious that any reporter had to be trained and, to be a good reporter, had somehow to acquire an objective approach to public problems. Among the intellectual youth (and this is whence reporters come, by and large), the acceptance of objectivity was all too hard to find anywhere; in the black community the intellectuals at least had cause to be bitter and subjective.

But this black approach of "quotas," even as represented by thoughtful and philosophical blacks, offered a very real danger to press freedom in the 1970s. Sterling Tucker, the executive director of the Washington Urban League and a member of the District of Columbia City Council, stated the position for quotas very well. Once he had opposed them. In 1972, he favored them, as a part of the solution to the black dilemma of publicity. "I found," he said, "that the only way to establish goals was to translate them into something measurable. Numbers is an easy and reasonable way to engage in quantitative measurement. . . . I know that many people see the use of this kind of racial quota as discrimination in reverse . . . quotas alone cannot be the whole thing. They can serve, at best, as one part of a process or a plan."

Tucker and other blacks had long felt that the black position, black feelings, were not properly represented in a white press. He visited the Far East and when he talked to people and leaders he noted that their opinions were derived from the white press and that "much of that opinion has to do with the blacks, and most of it is erroneous." Said Tucker,

I don't know that a black reporter can interpret me any better than a white reporter, but I would feel better if there were enough around to check each other out on matters which concern all of us. It is not that I don't think white folks can't understand me, it is just that they haven't given themselves much opportunity to know about me.

The seven blacks who filed the suit against the Washington *Post* had an even more vigorous position. They said that whites could not interpret blacks, and thus the *Post* ought to be giving that interpretive job to blacks.

Therein lies the danger to freedom: the acceptance of the thesis that white, black, Chinese, Japanese, Chicano, Puerto Rican, all have different "interpretabilities" that must in each case be handled by persons from precisely the same mold—which is to say that a Chicano reporter could not tell the truth about blacks. To carry it further, a Jewish reporter could not write correctly about Christians, a homosexual reporter could not write honestly of heterosexuals, a woman reporter could not write honestly of men, a man reporter could not write honestly of women.

Such internal threats to freedom of the press are very real, and they concern basically the aging process of what threatens to become "an institution," as more and more cities become one-newspaper towns. Various solutions have been offered within the profession of journalism and have been aired in such thoughtful magazines as the *Columbia Journalism Quarterly*, which is totally dedicated to the study and improvement of the trade. (One of journalism's basic problems is that it is part trade, part profession.)

For example, a proposal has been going the rounds of newspapering for the establishment of a national press council to adjudicate grievances against the press. But this idea brings hackles onto the necks of the tradesmen of journalism; they have no wish to be subjected to the same kind of restraints that medical societies and bar associations exercise over their membership. They want it both ways, and there lies another danger to the freedom of the press. The journalistic tradesmen say in effect: "We will not control ourselves, as a group. It is abhorrent that government control us. You must, Mr. and Ms. public, depend on our individual sense of ethics and fair play."

That is all very well, until the point when the public no longer believes, and then the newspapers are in serious trouble.

How close that point may be was indicated by Newbold Noyes, editor of the Washington *Star*, when he retired as president of the American Society of Newspaper Editors in 1971. Noyes suggested that the reason newspapers had lost the confidence of their readers was basically that the newspapers were not doing their job. "For one thing," he commented, "it is obvious that we are lazy and superficial in most of our reporting." He called attention to the case of the Black Panthers and the American press—a sad little paragraph in the history of journalism. During the 1960s, some twenty-eight Black Panthers were killed in confrontations with the police. Advocates of the Panthers claimed that these twenty-eight were "murdered." Much of the American press picked up the charge (made by a Panther attorney) and circulated it throughout the land. Then it was shown, by an investigative reporter who was really not a reporter at all but a graduate student making a study, that the Panther charge was exaggerated. The press had accepted a "handout" and printed it as fact without any reportorial investigation.

"Well," said Editor Noyes, "I have long ago stopped being amazed at my own inertia and stupidity, but I am *truly* amazed to find that all my fellow editors were, on this particular story, as inert and stupid as I."

Noyes said then that 80 per cent of the space of the newspapers was devoted to stereotyped happenings, and worse, that "news" was made only by application of stereotyped standards. The very word "stereotype" is a newspaper word, referring to the process by which type, arranged in forms by printers, is copied on a paper matrix placed on the type, and the impression of the type is transferred to a tubular or circular metal casting that fits on the press and actually prints the newspaper. "Stereotype" is a good word for newspaper work of the editorial variety in the 1970s; as they are stereotyped mechanically, so have the newspapers also become heavily stereotyped editorially.

"Newspaper readers," said Noyes, "need and deserve the information, the understanding, which will permit them to sort out the forces at work in society and decide where their true interests lie."

Elsewhere, he said:

Today our reflex action to the sensational statement, the thing that goes wrong, the anomaly—our reflex action to the man-bites-dog thing insures that the man will, indeed, bite the dog if he wants to get on page one. In this process of letting the kooks on both sides determine for us what constitutes tomorrow's news—and the kookier their activity the bigger the news—in this process, I say, we are giving our readers a view of society and its problems that *even we know to be false* [italics the authors']. Can we blame our readers for sensing that something is wrong with our performance?

And for once an editor recognized the nature of the challenge, for Noyes said that if the newspapers failed, as they were failing in 1972, the whole concept of the American scene was bound to change. There was the danger to freedom of the press—internally—in the 1970s, and it meant danger to the whole fabric of American society.

CHAPTER 4

The Special Problems of Believability

One day in the summer of 1972 Newspaper Columnist Norton Mockridge declared himself to be in a state of cataleptic despondency. The cause: his discovery of the results of a poll of "believability" taken by psychologists at the University of Connecticut. In this poll newspaper columnists ranked sixteenth in believability in a field of twenty, positioned between the TV repairman and the auto mechanic. The used-car salesman ranked last, and just ahead of him was the politician.

Mockridge made light of the problem, because that is the kind of columnist he is, but it was not very funny to the newspaper profession. ASNE President Newbold Noyes, as noted earlier, took much sadder note of the low estate to which journalism had receded.

The public's decreasing respect for the printed media's credibility had developed over a period of years. Virtually none of the public's present cynicism regarding the American press was evident at the end of World War II. To be sure there had always been cries of "unfair," but the leaders of journalism believed firmly in objectivity at that time, and by and large the newspapers were attempting to conform to high standards of objectivity. But there were erosions over the years.

In 1948, for example, when Harry Truman ran for a term

as President in his own right against Republican Thomas E. Dewey, the vast majority of the press both supported Dewey and predicted he would win the election. In fact, on election night, the Chicago *Tribune* announced in a huge front-page headline that Dewey had won. And then Truman won. The shock was tremendous in the newspaper industry, almost as serious as had been the shock when the *Literary Digest* had so wrongly predicted the victory of Alf Landon over Franklin D. Roosevelt in 1936. The *Literary Digest* had then gone to pieces fast—abandoned by a readership that no longer believed—and was absorbed by *Time* in 1938.

The *Literary Digest's* readers lost faith in it because of a public opinion poll, and in the public opinion poll must lie some of the seeds of reader rebellion in the 1970s.

The *Literary Digest* was more or less parent to the political opinion poll. It began taking "straw votes" during the 1920s by polling various groups on various issues. In 1924 it mailed out 16.5 million ballots and predicted that Coolidge would win the Presidential race. He did. Although the poll was full of error, the result came out all right, and in 1928 the *Digest* editors ran another poll that correctly, if with a large margin of error, predicted Herbert Hoover's election to the Presidency. The magazine had been conducting other polls, as well. In 1922, 1930, and 1932, for example, it polled public opinion on prohibition and found, quite accurately as it turned out, that most Americans wanted to repeal the anti-drinking laws. Newspaper editors were becoming so convinced of the poll's reliability that some even suggested polls were as accurate as the actual voting on Election Day.

Then came 1932 and an even greater victory for the *Literary Digest* poll: the accurate prediction that Franklin D. Roosevelt would win the election. In 1936, carried away by confidence in its polling technique, the *Literary Digest* dropped all caution. It sent out 10 million ballots, received about 2 million returns, and on the basis of that return predicted that Landon would take four of every seven votes and must win the election. But Landon lost. The result: total disaster for the *Literary Digest*.

The *Literary Digest* did not fail simply because it was wrong on a public opinion poll, however. The magazine had already lost much ground to two weekly newsmagazines, *Time* and *Newsweek*, which presented fresh ideas in a fresh setting. The loss of reader confidence cannot be overemphasized, however.

Over the years, opinion polls gained back much of their prestige when new pollsters with new techniques—Elmo Roper, George Gallup, and later, Louis Harris—entered the field. The 1948 disaster, in which virtually all newspapers and virtually all polls predicted the Dewey victory, caused much soul-searching among press and pollsters. Out of it came more care, but in some cases vacillation and hedging, which did nothing to build up reader confidence.

Still, with the increase in consolidations in the 1950s, the press prospered. But it was during the fifties, too, that the social scene was undergoing radical change, and the newspapers found themselves out of step with the times.

The changes were vast. In the 1940s virtually no newspaper would print picture and story of a black couple's wedding. For example, at the Washington *Evening Star,* black news was no news in 1943, in spite of Washington's huge black community. If there was violence in a black neighborhood, it had to be excessive to rate even a paragraph in the newspaper. City editors prided themselves on knowing, even to the city block, which areas of Washington were white, which were black—and sent reporters out on stories accordingly. Black news was almost never covered.

By 1972 all newspapers in America were running pictures and stories of black weddings, Chicano weddings—all weddings—as a routine matter. But so rapid was social change that in the eyes of community members the newspaper was not keeping up. Blacks still did not believe in the reliability of the press to cover black activity—thus the surge of black publications, even to a black news service in Washington. Other minorities felt the same way. Even those who had not considered themselves as among the minorities began to share the same feelings of exclusion: the middle-class workers of Caucasion extraction, for example, felt that their interests were being ignored by a press that was toadying to the minorities.

In such a situation the press could not hope to win the skirmishes, and if it was to win the war, it must adopt a strong, morally defensible position. But the press in the 1970s was running scared; it was more likely to respond to pinpricks than before.

The attacks came from many sides. Leonard Bernstein, the composer and conductor, speaking to the National Press Club in Washington, said, "I've become very wary of the press. . . . I keep reading about myself and not recognizing myself. . . . Not only am I misquoted by the yard, but also misrepresented."

The whole Washington press was hurt in the spring of 1972 when Representative Benjamin Rosenthal of New York demanded a Congressional investigation of the *Post* and the *Star*—for their advertising policies. A cooperative supermarket chain had tried to place a full-page advertisement in the newspapers, challenging the big supermarket chains with not doing enough to promote lower food prices. The newspapers had refused to run the ad. Explanations aside, and there were reasons for it that could be argued both ways, the net result was a lessening of the public faith in even the advertising content of the newspapers.

Nick Williams, retired editor of the Los Angeles *Times,* claimed in an article that crime and violence did *not* sell newspapers, and that newspapers had long since passed the stage at which crime and violence reporting did build circulation. The average reader in America was not inclined to believe Williams's remark, or his avowal that newspapers were better than ever, that they did a finer job—even though there is evidence that what he said is true.

One reason, again, is opinion polls. The polls have come from everywhere, in recent years, and many newspapers have seen fit to publish them—so many that in 1968 the American Association for Public Opinion Research sent every newspaper in the country a warning against indiscriminate use of polls. In 1972, Mayor John Lindsay of New York used a poll to try to convince the public that he was running well in Florida. He ran very badly. The poll had been highly played up by the Miami *Herald* (a Knight newspaper) and by *Newsweek.* Some readers were bound to remember.

By 1972, newspapers were wary of polls. The more responsible papers were careful to follow standards laid down by the Association for Public Opinion Research. But not all did.

Obvious unfairness of the news media was noted very broadly in 1972. Senator Henry M. Jackson of Washington brought one case to the public eye. During the Florida Democratic primary campaign, the Associated Press dispatched a news photograph that showed Senator Jackson in a Florida park with apparently only two people listening as he spoke: a boy on a bicycle and a woman. It was a pathetic picture, symbolizing the efforts of the failing politician to attract a crowd and his determination to plunge on, even in the face of disaster. It said all those things to the newspaper reader.

Senator Jackson cried "foul." He produced another picture, taken from behind him, showing those two people as well as a very respectable crowd *behind them.* The AP's photographer had obviously sacrificed good journalism for, in his opinion, a good picture. Many of the people who saw the two pictures in juxtaposition, but only *after* Jackson had complained—they would remember.

Another aspect of the "unbelievable" character of the general press has been its failure to stand up for the freedom rights of all. The Twentieth Century Fund report on press freedom showed that there was no editorial outcry from the general press over mistreatment of the underground press. When the Los Angeles *Free Press* people were tried for receiving stolen goods, the Los Angeles *Times* did not comment until *after* the conviction and never did discuss the matter of the First Amendment. Few newspapers came to the defense of Ralph Ginzburg, publisher of *Eros,* who went to jail after a long fight over his publication of various pictures the courts called prurient and his use of the U.S. mails to pander to pruriency. The pictures Ginzburg published certainly had to be compared with the outright sex pictures in the underground press, but the Ginzburg case did not arouse newspaper editorialists to fury.

Even more inexplicable, if freedom is really to exist for all, was the failure of the American press to take strong issue with the expulsion of two Taiwanese journalists by Secretary General U Thant of the United Nations because the Peking government asked for the expulsion. The excuse was that the Central News Agency of Taiwan was controlled by the Taiwanese government. But it had always been so controlled. Tass was controlled by the Soviet government. The New China News Agency, accredited with Peking's joining the

UN, was controlled by Peking. What the UN said in effect was that there was not to be freedom of the press at the United Nations. And the American press swallowed it without a whisper of protest. Those who interested themselves in UN news remembered.

More exciting by far than these cases was the issue raised by Columnist Jack Anderson in 1972 with the leaking of secret information from the highest councils of the American government during a world crisis.

Jack Anderson inherited the old Drew Pearson shock column in 1969, when Pearson died. The column was carried in 700 American newspapers, but after some two years in which Anderson came up with no major "exposures" of the kind that made Pearson famous, there was some question in Washington gossip circles whether Anderson would "make" it. Although he was indefatigable in his muckraking, he was often dead wrong. In a column in 1969 he charged flatly that Donald Rumsfeld, director of the Office of Economic Opportunity, had diverted funds from the poor to embellish his private office with expensive furnishings, even a private bathroom. The story proved to be total fabrication. There had been *no* redecoration at OEO. The matter was brought up in the Congress and made its way into the record. Anderson went to the OEO office, found that he was wrong, but he never did run a correction. Nor did any Washington newspaper or any other reporters see fit to make the truth generally known. Since the untruth had been told in some 700 newspapers, and very blatantly in many of them, it hardly seemed fair or responsible to withhold the truth from the public. Some people who learned the facts, they would remember.

Then, on January 4, 1972, the Washington *Post* received three secret documents from the National Security Council. The source was Jack Anderson. He was writing columns about the material, and wanted the fullest possible publicity. The *Post* gave the Anderson story all the "ride" it would take in the old-fashioned newspaper way. The matter aroused national uproar and controversy, and Jack Anderson's reputation was made in his own right for the first time.

The secret papers concerned the India-Pakistan crisis of 1971, the war that followed, and the American attitude to it all. The United States had taken a strong stand against India's invasion and conquest of East Pakistan. Anderson's purloined papers showed how, in part, Presidential Adviser Henry Kissinger had conducted himself at various meetings and what had been said. It was very clearly a violation of the confidence of the executive branch, by someone who apparently had not agreed with the policy.

It was embarrassing to the government to be exposed in the process of making policy, for in that process, all opinions and avenues were explored, and some opinions and some ways of stating them were not very complimentary to some of the parties concerned. Some charged (Anderson led in this) that the administration had led the country down the garden path and had lied. About that charge, the Washington *Star* (which did not run the Anderson column, the *Post* did) raised some questions, particularly about the ability of any administration to keep secrets. Then the *Star* said this about the viability of the Anderson claims:

The charge of some critics that these memoranda show that the administration misled the public in the course of the India-Pakistan crisis is inevitable, and in our view quite untenable. . . . On the contrary, whether or not one agrees with the administration's decisions during this period, the secret documents establish convincingly that they were rational decisions, taken after careful deliberation.

In the eyes of many, the Anderson "scandal" was no more than an attention-getting process. Anderson made the most of it. "Why I Blew the Whistle" was the title of the article he wrote for *Parade,* a newspaper Sunday supplement. The Washington *Post* declared that "we can all be grateful to Jack Anderson, who has brought to the public's attention material essential to the public's understanding."

But there were other points of view. In Congress, some members took seriously the problem of trying to protect private government discussions from theft and delivery to the press. Columnist James Kilpatrick, a conservative, noted that "we must infer . . . that someone still employed at the very highest level of public confidence . . . has wantonly violated the trust reposed in him. This goes beyond disloyalty, it sails close to the windward edge of treason. . . ."

Tom Braden, not a conservative, writing in the editorial pages of the Washington *Post,* warned that the net result might be to make advisers too careful of what they said in meetings: "To reduce men to such choice makes a mockery of government. Nobody will argue against the public's right to know the logic behind its foreign policy. But the difference between reporting the making of foreign policy and reporting private conversations is the difference between the reporter and the spy."

Strong words.

Tom Wicker of *The New York Times* had strong words the other way: "It took years for someone to challenge that arrogant privilege (security classification), in the case of the Viet Nam war; but it has happened much more quickly in the India-Pakistan case. Maybe the government is now finding its own officials less willing to let deception and ineptitude be shrouded in 'security.' "

The furor died down. Had the press let the matter die, it

would have. But the Pulitzer committee awarded Jack Anderson a special prize for his India-Pakistan "scoop," and that revived all the controversy surrounding the issue.

Anderson's reliability was brought further into question in the summer of 1972 when he charged, totally without factual evidence, that Senator Thomas Eagleton had been arrested on numerous occasions for drunken driving. Eagleton was then Democratic vice-presidential nominee and under fire within his own party because he had been treated in a mental hospital earlier in his career and had not indicated that when presidential candidate George McGovern selected him as his running mate.

McGovern had been inclined to forgive Eagleton's lapse, but that was before the Anderson "exposé." Anderson's unsubstantiated disclosures about Eagleton proved totally false and groundless, and Anderson was forced to apologize publicly for his fakery. But the Anderson jab had been a final straw that forced Eagleton's removal from the ticket.

One thing was certain: Anderson would never again have the power and the credibility that he had enjoyed before the Eagleton incident. The whole episode was an abysmal example of the wrongful exercise of press power by a reporter, and it exposed yet another reason for the public's loss of confidence in the press and another danger to press freedom: sneakiness and excesses.

Some Americans had been aware for a long time of the serious damage that newspapers could cause. During World War II a Chicago *Tribune* journalist's "scoop" of unbelievable irresponsibility had cost America thousands of lives. The story concerned the Japanese naval codes.

In the spring of 1942, when America's situation in the war against Japan was desperate, the Japanese decided to invade Midway Island and the Aleutians and set up bases that might lead to the capture of Hawaii and perhaps further incursions against the American mainland. At the very least, the United States fleet stood a good chance of being completely destroyed.

In May 1942 Admiral Nimitz's intelligence officers succeeded in breaking the Japanese naval code. As a result, Nimitz learned of the invasion of Midway and the force involved, and he was able to forestall it with a much smaller carrier force under Admiral Raymond Spruance and win the battle. The American Navy now had the very valuable advantage of being able to tell what the Japanese were going to do and when. But all this was blown sky-high when a Chicago *Tribune* reporter, learning that the United States had broken the Japanese code, sent a story back to Chicago, and the Chicago *Tribune* editors printed it. The Japanese immediately changed their code, the United States could no longer read it, and the war, obviously, was lengthened—all because of an irresponsible action that was very nearly treasonable.

A Gallup poll in July 1971 showed that most Americans wanted freedom of the press and that many people were concerned about it. The poll also showed, however, that 56 per cent of the American people felt the press was too quick to publish classified information without consideration of its effect on the national security and that 57 per cent felt national security might be violated by such disclosures.

CHAPTER 5

The Pentagon Papers

The erosion of public confidence in the printed media is important to the cause of their freedom because, if the public ceases to believe the press, freedom of speech and press are gradually bound to be eroded.

Officialdom at every level, by the very nature of its form and self-appointed tasks, is the enemy of a free press. Responsible public officials have long accepted the "antagonist" relationship of press and government as normal and necessary, but that does not mean that if the power of the press as deterrent is weakened, officialdom will not become officious.

Thus one of the great "victories" for freedom of the press, won in 1971 may turn out to have been a pyrrhic one at best. And at worst it has caused serious concerns among responsible journalists about their course in the future.

The case concerns the Pentagon Papers.

In 1971, Daniel Ellsberg, who had occupied a sensitive and trusted position as an employee of the Rand Corporation, which advises government at the highest levels, gave secret papers concerning the Vietnam war to the press.

For over a year Ellsberg had tried without success to interest Congress in the papers—he had sent them to the Senate Foreign Relations Committee, but they were ignored. Then, in the spring of 1971, a *New York Times'* correspondent, Neil Sheehan, received some of these papers, and one day in

June the *Times* began publishing excerpts from them. The next day, U.S. Attorney General John Mitchell asked the *Times* to stop publishing the papers and to return them to the government, all in the interest of national security. The *Times* refused, and the Department of Justice then obtained a restraining order and filed a civil suit seeking a permanent order, or injunction. When the court ruled in favor of the *Times,* the government appealed to the next highest judicial body, the U.S. Circuit Court. That court held that the *Times* could not publish material the government considered likely to endanger national security. The *Times* appealed to the U.S. Supreme Court, which held that the *Times* should be allowed to resume publication.

Meanwhile the Washington *Post* also secured copies of the classified information the government wanted held secret and began printing it. Nearly all other newspapers around the country followed suit, although none printed the stories in as much detail as did the *Times* and the *Post.*

The arguments of the Supreme Court justices, in their decisions on the cases, tell a good deal about the problems of freedom of the media in America. Associate Justice Hugo Black said that cases brought against the *Times* and the Washington *Post* represented "flagrant, indefensible, and continuing violation of the First Amendment." For the first time in one hundred and eighty-two years, said Justice Black, the federal courts were asked to hold that the First Amendment did not mean what it said, and that government could halt publication of "current news of vital importance to the people of the country."

Both the history and the language of the First Amendment, said the justice, support the view that the press must be left free to publish news, whatever the source, without censorship, injunctions, or prior restraints. Justice Black stated:

In the First Amendment the Founding Fathers gave the free press the protection it must have to fulfill its essential role in our democracy. The press was to serve the governed, not the governors. The Government's power to censor the press was abolished so that the press would remain forever free to censure the Government. The press was protected so that it could bare the secrets of government and inform the people. Only a free and unrestrained press can effectively expose deception in government. And paramount among the responsibilities of a free press is the duty to prevent any part of the government from deceiving the people and sending them off to distant lands to die of foreign fevers and foreign shot and shell. In my view, far from deserving condemnation for their courageous reporting, *The New York Times* and the Washington *Post* and other newspapers should be commended for serving the purpose that the Founding Fathers saw so clearly. In revealing the workings of government that led to the Viet Nam war, the newspapers nobly did precisely that which the Founders hoped and trusted they would do.

In a concurring opinion, Justice William O. Douglas quoted a decision by former Chief Justice Charles Evans Hughes, which had a strong bearing on this case:

While reckless assaults upon public men, and efforts to bring obloquy upon these who are endeavoring faithfully to discharge official duties, exert a baleful influence and deserve the severest condemnation in public opinion, it cannot be said that this abuse is greater, and it is believed to be less, than that which characterized the period in which our institutions took shape.

Hughes there was referring to the trials of the Founding Fathers and to their attitude toward the press. President George Washington, as noted earlier, frequently charged the press of his day with printing lies about his administration and trying to wreck everything he did. He spoke of the press's "outrages against common decency" and "willful and malignant misrepresentation" and warned that if the course of conduct of the press was allowed to continue, it would become impossible to govern the country.

John Adams, the second President, never forgot the "narrow bigotry, the most envious malignity, the most base, vulgar, sordid, fishwoman scurrility" of the American press. Thomas Jefferson, lionized by the press at the beginning, soon began to talk about the "evil for which there is no remedy" and the journalists' habit of "mutilating whatever they can get hold of," and Jefferson warned that "these abuses of an institution so important to freedom and sciences, are deeply to be regretted, inasmuch as they tend to lessen its usefulness, and to sap its safety."

From the same opinion of Chief Justice Hughes, Justice Douglas went on to quote a further passage that seemed even more applicable to the Pentagon Papers case:

The administration of government has become more complex, the opportunities for malfeasance and corruption have multiplied, crime has grown to most serious proportions, and the danger of its protection by unfaithful officials and of the impairment of the fundamental security of life and property by criminal alliances and official neglect, emphasize the primary need of a vigilant and courageous press, especially in great cities. The fact that the liberty of the press may be abused by miscreant purveyors of scandal does not make any the less necessary the immunity of the press from previous restraint in dealing with official misconduct.

And Justice Douglas, for himself, said, "Secrecy in government is fundamentally anti-democratic, perpetuating bureaucratic errors. Open debate and discussion of public issues are vital to our national health."

Justice Potter Stewart, also concurred in the decision—because he could not say that disclosure of these documents would result in "irreparable" damage to the nation, and that being so, the First Amendment certainly applied. But Justice Stewart also struck a note of warning:

It is elementary that the successful conduct of international diplomacy and the maintenance of an effective national defense require both confidentiality and secrecy. Other nations can hardly deal with this Nation in an atmosphere of mutual trust unless they can be sure that their confidences will be kept. And within our own executive departments, the development of considered and intelligent international policies would be impossible if those charged with their formulation could not communicate with each other freely, frankly, and in confidence.

Associate Justice Byron White added to this warning: "Nor, after examining the materials the Government characterizes as the most sensitive and destructive, can I deny that revelation of these documents will do substantial damage to public interests. Indeed, I am confident that the disclosure will have that result."

(One of the plaints of the government, which military men saw as extremely serious, was that the publication of messages that had been carried by radio in code would give foreign governments the opportunity to read the American messages sent abroad in those codes for months or even perhaps years back. It was the practice of various government intelligence agencies the world around to monitor radio broadcasts. All that other government agencies need do, given enough texts of coded messages, was to compare them against the coded texts, and the codes would be broken.)

In spite of his serious reservations, Justice White concurred with the majority decision, because the law specifically stated the rights of the press to be safe from "prior restraint" of publication of materials. Justice White also pointed out that this right did not prevent the government from bringing criminal sanctions against an irresponsible press.

The government did not exercise that right against the newspapers that published the Pentagon Papers, but it did bring Daniel Ellsberg to trial. The results of that trial will, of course, determine the future course of other potential violators of government confidence.

Chief Justice Burger, Justice Harlan, and Justice Blackmun dissented from the majority view. The Chief Justice rejected the "absolute" nature of the First Amendment and lamented the "unseemly haste" of the whole proceeding. He wrote in his dissent:

The newspapers make a derivative claim under the First Amendment. They denominate this right as the public right-to-know; by implication, the *Times* asserts a sole trusteeship of that right by virtue of its journalistic "scoop." The right is asserted as an absolute. Of course, the First Amendment right itself is not an absolute, as Justice Holmes so long ago pointed out in his aphorism concerning the right to shout of fire in a crowded theater. . . . There are no doubt other exceptions no one has had occasion to describe or discuss. . . . A great issue of this kind should be tried in a judicial atmosphere conducive to thoughtful, reflective deliberation.

And here was the crux of Chief Justice Burger's dissent:

Would it have been unreasonable, since the newspaper could anticipate the government's objections to release of secret material, to give the government an opportunity to review the entire collection and determine whether agreement could be reached on publication? Stolen or not, if security was not in fact jeopardized, much of the material could no doubt have been declassified, since it spans a period ending in 1968. With such an approach—one that great newspapers have in the past practiced and stated editorially to be the duty of an honorable press—the newspapers and government might well have narrowed the area of disagreement as to what was and was not publishable, leaving the remainder to be resolved in orderly litigation if necessary. To me it is hardly believable that a newspaper long regarded as a great institution in American life would fail to perform one of the basic and simple duties of every citizen with respect to the discovery or possession of stolen property or secret government documents.

In their dissent statements Justices Harlan and Blackmun also cited the unseemly haste of publication and the responsibility of the press in the matter. Justice Blackmun put it this way:

If, however, damage has been done, and if, with the Court's action today, these newspapers proceed to publish the critical documents and there results therefrom the "death of soldiers, the destruction of alliances, the greatly increased difficulty of negotiation with our enemies, the inability of our diplomats to negotiate," to which list I might add the factors of prolongation of the war and of further delay in freeing of United States prisoners, then the Nation's people will know where the responsibility for these sad consequences rests.

The *Times* and the *Post* won their case. Of course they crowed loudly, and much of the American press crowed with them, about the victory they had won over the forces of government which were attempting to restrain the press in its absolute exercise of the First Amendment. The Pulitzer Prize committee, in fact, gave *The New York Times* a prize, in 1972, for its exposé of the Pentagon Papers. At best these were purloined papers, secured by a reporter from a trusted government-connected worker who had violated his own word in revealing matters of state. Had the federal government not overreacted, perhaps matters would have been different. But the Pulitzer Prize to *The New York Times* seemed more an act of defiance of the Presidency than an award—and thus the award became politicized.

All the facts of the Pentagon Papers matter would be a long time in coming in; many would probably not be known for years. But some facts were known, even in the immediate aftermath. Most important of them was the state of affairs between government and press that had led to the "unseemly haste."

Relations between government and the press had been deteriorating steadily since the Eisenhower administration (see Chapter 14 "The Government and the Media"). But they had never been as bad as they were in the Nixon administration. One reason for this, of course, was the conservative nature of the Nixon administration. The *Times* and the *Post* tended to disagree with Walter Lippmann, who held that an administration like this, a breathing spell after forty years of almost uninterrupted liberalism with money and ideas, was essential to the welfare of the nation. The liberal press regarded the Nixon administration as retrogressive in nature, which did not help in the matter of rational discussions of the Pentagon Papers. Nor did the press's impatience with an unpopular war help, either, and if President Nixon could claim that it was not his war, that he was winding it down where everyone before him had wound it up, popular opinion still held that too soon was not fast enough.

The disturbing aspects of the Pentagon Papers case were brought out by various concerned newspapermen. Lester Markel, for many years Sunday editor of *The New York Times,* held that the real issue was not one of national security or press freedom, but the issue of press responsibility. "This is not a legal but an ethical matter and on that score I think the news media can be faulted," wrote Markel in his book *What You Don't Know Can Hurt You.* In further discussion, Markel indicated that Admiral U. S. Grant Sharp, commander in the Pacific during part of the war, made the point that the Pentagon Papers were written by biased persons. "Slant was piled upon slant," as Markel said, assessing Sharp's remarks. Markel had other opinions: that the disclosures were not important enough to create all the fuss; that a newspaper does not have a "right" to protect its sources if the government has no such right.

According to the Gallup poll conducted in the summer of 1971 (referred to in an earlier chapter), 57 per cent of the persons polled reacted with the feeling that security had been harmed, while 48 per cent disapproved of the government's action in trying to control the papers and 34 per cent felt that freedom of the press had been violated by the government.

What remained to be seen, and it would be seen in time, was the harm or good that had come from the action. The *Times* and the *Post* had established their "right" to declassify and print any documents they could get their hands on. But let them be wrong, let the public be convinced that the press was arrogating government responsibility and indeed endangering the American people, and the nation would undoubtedly support the strongest restrictions on the press, even to the abrogation of the basic freedom of the First Amendment. That was the danger the press was running in printing state secrets.

CHAPTER 6

The Underground Press

To some extent, the underground press has been as much a part of America as the general press. There has always been a press of discontent in America, but never had it flourished more than in the 1960s and 1970s.

The alternate press could, like the established press, go through different phases and major changes. For example, twenty years earlier, the local newspaper of Greenwich Village in New York City was the *Villager,* a comfortable, staid newspaper that published news notes and reports of events and people in this homey area of New York. But in the middle 1950s, a group of young dissidents, of whom Norman Mailer was one, began publishing an "alternate" newspaper, the *Village Voice.* The *Voice* was filled with articles intending to break down the old mores: homosexuality was spoken of openly; the "establishment" was roundly lampooned in Jules Feiffer's cartoons and in the columns of various writers. The *Voice* prospered and the *Villager* faded. And then the *Voice* became, in its own way, a symbol of "the establishment." The young and the artistic poor tended to move over to the East Village or down to New York's Lower East Side, and Greenwich Village became a high-rent district. A new "alternate" newspaper, the *East Village Other,* began publishing. In the 1960s the *Other* was marked by free use of four-letter words, as the courts decided ever more leniently on censorship and obscenity. Soon this paper began running what earlier would have been called "filthy" pictures and cartoons. Meanwhile, the *Village Voice,* having achieved a circulation of 200,000 copies, had become a "fat cat."

Mores and newspapers changed with the times. What had shocked one generation in the *Village Voice* caused the next to say ho-hum. The radical, or underground press, as always, tended either to become part of the establishment or to fade away.

In general, the underground press of the seventies came in two varieties, the political press and the sexual press. Basically speaking, too, the sexual press was an exercise in pornography. Encouraged by several court decisions of the late 1960s and early 1970s against censorship of materials that earlier would have been found obscene, the sexual press printed photographs of genitalia, and it featured cartoons and articles dealing with sex activity in all its aberrations. This sexual press fought an almost constant battle against all kinds of censorship, from the action of law officers seeking injunctions in various localities to the flat refusal of some news dealers to handle the materials and the pressures of church groups and other organizations against their sale.

One of the underground press papers, the San Francisco *Ball,* had this to say in justification of the sex press: "We are and plan to remain a counter-culture publication concerned about and commenting on the problems and pressures of a new sexual life style. We are not a tabloid for the collectors of bicycle seats nor have we any desire to be the object of masturbative orgasm in the sweaty hand of a fourteen-year-old kid. The *Ball* is aimed at the sexually freed young adult who doesn't get up-tight when he . . . reads a four letter word."

A justification of the underground press was made by the

American Civil Liberties Union. Aryeh Neier, ACLU executive director, characterized the alternate press as a force which works against self-censorship in the establishment press: "It is a part of the purpose and the effect of much of the 'alternate' press to serve as a gadfly to the 'establishment' press."

A serious problem of the underground press has always been government harassment, and in recent years this has provided many cases for the ACLU. Such papers have been barred from military bases, prisons, and high schools. In 1970-71 some sixty college papers were censored. Still, instead of diminishing, ACLU in 1972 believed the underground press was flourishing and becoming more aggressive in its use of its First Amendment rights.

After the 1968 Democratic convention in Chicago, which produced so much violence, a new kind of newspaper made its appearance. This was the working journalists' own newspaper, published by newspapermen who were dissatisfied with the standard newspaper coverage. The Chicago *Journalism Review* was possibly the earliest of these. Others appeared elsewhere: in Washington, D.C., for example. Often they were harried, officials tending to see in them forces of revolution. Two Washington papers, for example, the Washington *Free Press* and the *Quicksilver Times,* were subject to some 300 incidents of harassment by the District of Columbia police, and the *Quicksilver Times* suspended operations in the summer of 1972.

Just how dangerous did these underground papers tend to be? Perhaps a quick study of one issue of one paper may give a clue.

The *Straight Creek Journal* was an underground newspaper published in Denver as "a living experiment in journalism aimed at reforming the concept of community newspapers."

In its issue of May 25, 1972, the lead article discussed the coming festival of the Universal Life Church and Rainbow Family Tribe, which was planned for the Granby-Grand Lake area that summer, and the difficulties of the organizers with state authorities. The article was straightforward, telling the story of the efforts of the group to plan, and the efforts of some government officials to discourage the meeting. It was editorial in tone: "This summer the people of Colorado will have a very fine opportunity to see how far our state officials will go to prevent citizens from holding outdoor festivals in the Rocky Mountains, . . . but if responsible preparations are made by the festival organizers and technicalities of the new resolutions are used to break up the event, the citizens of Colorado will have a good example of how the 'power to regulate' can be used to deny constitutional rights."

This newspaper was trading on what the ACLU called the public sense of suspicion of the news purveyed in the establishment press. No more than that.

Another article dealt with a grand jury investigation in the nearby town of Boulder of the beatings of Dr. Philip Thompson and his family during an antiwar riot. Another was about the case of a health-food saleswoman, harried for practicing medicine without a license. There was also an interview with Chief of Police Arthur Dill of Denver, concerned with enforcement of laws about hitchhiking and drugs, for the most part. Several articles were devoted to antiwar matters, including one that told in detail of a demonstrator who threw blood on an army colonel at Ft. Carson. The articles, by and large, were intelligent and reasonable. The advertisements, unlike those in the sex-oriented underground papers, were "straight" for the most part.

What seemed apparent was that the underground press

was more diverse than the establishment press. There were about 300 underground papers in the U.S. in 1972, plus perhaps another 200 that appeared sporadically in mimeograph. As for influence, they had perhaps a million readers, among the young and "activists" for the most part. They could create response, as in 1968 and thereafter, in the Chicago demonstrations and trials, when they almost uniformly called for protests and were heard and answered by groups around the country.

The harrying of these publications has taken various forms. Some called it harrying when Vice President Agnew spoke up against the underground press, which he did in a speech in 1970. Senator Thomas J. Dodd of Connecticut later that year introduced a bill to prohibit publications that advocated violence against law-enforcement men and overthrow of the government. That same year the Vermont Senate adopted a resolution calling for investigation of all underground newspapers in that state.

One reason for that kind of reaction to the underground press was that much of the material it published violated accepted public ideas. When the newspapers called the police "pigs," most people did not like it. Most people did not approve of the sexualism of many newspapers, either. So from the beginning the underground press forfeited any broad spectrum of American public support and was thus prey to its enemies and subject to the restraints of the courts.

In the summer of 1969, the Los Angeles *Free Press* published an official list of undercover California narcotics agents, complete with rank, home address, and telephone number of each. In other words, the paper "blew" the agents' cover and made them ineffectual in their jobs. Outraged authority stepped in. The California state legislature passed a law making publication of such a list a crime. But since it was not a crime when the *Free Press* published its list, Publisher Arthur Kynkin and Reporter Gerald Applebaum were tried and convicted of receiving stolen goods, for the list had been purloined by a clerk in the California state attorney's office. Kynkin and Applebaum were fined and were given probationary terms of three and five years, respectively.

Kynkin and Applebaum appealed, pointing out that in 1969 in Washington, D.C., Columnist Drew Pearson received from one of Senator Thomas Dodd's former employees documents purloined from the senator's files. What happened to Pearson? He became a hero. The suit against him was dismissed and the purloined documents were used in the Senate's case against Dodd that led to Dodd's censure and his subsequent defeat in his bid for reelection. Two standards? There seemed to be.

In 1968, Dallas police raided the underground newspaper Dallas *Notes* and carried away two tons of material including typewriters. The editor, Bret Stein, was charged with possession of pornography. Later, the case was thrown out of court.

In Buffalo, New York, in 1970, police drove the Black Panther newspaper off the streets by threatening to prosecute vendors for advocating overthrow of the government by force and violence. Seven street vendors were arrested. Also in Buffalo, staff members of the underground paper *Cold Steel* were indicted for criminal anarchy and incitement to riot. One issue had shown a picture of a burning school building, with the caption "back to school."

Another way of restricting the underground press has been to deny press credentials to reporters of these papers. In 1967 the Los Angeles authorities refused to issue police passes to the eight reporters of the *Free Press,* although this publication then had a weekly circulation of 85,000 copies. One reason given was that disaster scenes might become overcrowded with journalists. But Los Angeles issued 1,800 press cards each year to others. Another reason given was that the *Free Press* did not routinely cover police news. The Los Angeles action was upheld by the courts. The *Free Press* then took its case to the Supreme Court, and that body denied review, which had the effect of upholding the prior court's ruling.

In San Diego, when the underground newspaper *Street Journal* published a number of muckraking articles about banking practices in the area, the newspaper's offices were attacked several times. The editors considered this harassment and suspected it when the crimes went unsolved.

In Milwaukee the editor of *Kaleidoscope* was found guilty under a new law against obscenity, which he said was written especially to prosecute this paper. He was fined $2,000 and given two years' probation. His office and his car were also bombed. Later, in 1970, *Kaleidoscope* was again in trouble when it ran a statement from a group that claimed credit for the murderous bombing of the physics building at the University of Wisconsin. The editor was subpoenaed by a grand jury, refused to testify, and spent six months in jail for contempt.

In Atlanta the *Great Speckled Bird* considered itself harried when a local parents' league for decency started a leaflet campaign against it, to "put a stop to this flow of filth before it hurts the children more than it already has."

In St. Louis one of the editors of *Xanadu* protested that his freedom of the press was violated when he was arrested on a marijuana charge by a plainclothes policeman posing as a hippie.

Studying the underground press, among other things, in 1972, a Twentieth Century Fund task force came to the conclusion that the United States had two standards, one for the general press, and a much less secure guarantee of freedom under the First Amendment for the underground press. Its recommendation, not entirely agreeable to all its members, was that the underground press should have all legal and constitutional rights applicable to other sectors of the press, and that the rest of the press should especially protect the underground press. A dissenter felt that it should also be made clear that the underground press should be given only the same constitutional protections as the other press and no special position in such matters as search and seizure. But all the members of the task force agreed that the underground press, whatever its intrinsic worth, was a part of the press and should have all the protections of the First Amendment.

CHAPTER 7

Newsmagazines and Weeklies

The one great innovation in the American printed media of the twentieth century has been the newsmagazines, which were founded on the idea that by the 1920s the American people had become too busy to read newspapers. The success, then, of *Time,* and later of *Newsweek* and *U.S. News & World Report* attests to this idea as a sound publishing principle in respect to American society.

When Briton Hadden and Henry R. Luce offered their prospectus for *Time* to investors and advertisers in 1922, they made no claims against newspapers or any of the existing publications. They said simply that information was not getting through. They proved it with the success and growth of *Time,* until in the 1970s the newsmagazines occupied a respected and substantial place in the field of journalism.

Time started out with a cheerful admission of bias and the hunch of the editors that objectivity was impossible. The opinions of the editors, worked neatly into the news articles, brought about success, but also a certain dissatisfaction with the opinions thus presented. The result was the establishment of *Newsweek,* in the 1930s, as a sort of counterbalance. There proved to be room for both, the more prosaic, carefully "noneditorial" *Newsweek* and the opinionated, livelier *Time.*

Both magazines indulge in so-called group journalism: the

articles they publish are the result of many talents working together. Researchers and writers and editors of the various sections of the magazines hold weekly meetings at which the news of current interest is discussed, and a slate of possible stories is drawn up. The researcher then queries the various magazine bureaus in areas throughout the country or "stringers" who serve regions without full-fledged bureaus. Thus material is gathered from afar in addition to what can be dug up through local interviews and research. A voluminous amount of material is collected.

A writer will write the story. Then it must go to his or her immediate editor, who makes what changes he or she wishes. The article is then sent to the managing editor, who may want material added or deleted or the article completely rewritten. Each person has contributed to the article. The final viewpoint or stress, however, will inevitably rest with the managing editor.

Researchers will dot the words in the copy, indicating that their accuracy has been checked. They will also dot opinion, for opinion belongs to the editor and cannot really be verified or challenged.

A quarter century ago, *Time* was considered full of opinion, albeit unsigned opinion, and *Newsweek* prided itself on being the "factual" magazine. Today the positions are not reversed, but *Newsweek* tends also to express opinion along with newsworthy items. Both magazines now have loosened their policy of anonymity by featuring a number of signed articles, giving credit for the views of the writer. But, as with newspapers, bias on various issues on the part of both of these newsmagazines is evident and, one supposes, unavoidable.

A few years after *Newsweek* began publication, David Lawrence, a successful Washington columnist, started another kind of magazine, *U.S. News,* which consisted largely of "stories-in-depth," that is to say, longer articles devoted to the news event in question, with a background approach to it. Then came an attempt to begin a world news magazine (as America began to see itself as a world power). The result was *World Report,* which did not flourish so well; but when combined with *U.S. News,* the publication did indeed meet a need.

Other specialized news publications rose and fell. One of the most successful, the *Kiplinger Reports,* which developed out of the newsletter of another Washington correspondent, was unique in that it could not be received other than through the mail, for it could only be purchased by subscription. Unique and in a sense foolhardy, for any change in the special mailing privileges normally held by magazines and newspapers was a threat to the freedom of the printed press. And in the 1970s the threat was real, indeed: Congress, on the urgings of a deficit-ridden postal system, was seriously considering the imposition of new high rates for the mailing of news media.

For nearly two hundred years the United States government had recognized the special responsibility of the Post Office to bind the nation together. The principle followed was that the postal service had a job other than simply distributing the mails. The job was, as a Special Congressional Commission said in 1844: "to render the citizen worthy, by proper knowledge and enlightenment, of his important privileges as a sovereign constituent of his government; to diffuse enlightenment and social improvement. . . ."

Thus the Post Office traditionally gave newspapers and magazines a postage rate, under the special second-class mailing privileges, that would make it possible for the publishers to reach a large audience at a minimal fee. Indeed, in the county of publication, newspapers were mailed *without charge.*

But after years of unbalanced budgets, deficit financing, and almost constant complaint about the Post Office as a "bad manager," both executive and legislative branches of government had become sensitive. Further, the rise of television, it could be argued, had made the special privileges of the printed press unnecessary. So various bills were introduced into Congress which would slash the special second-class mailing privileges that had controlled the relations of press and Post Office. Then, in August 1970, the United States Post Office Department was reorganized by act of Congress as the United States Postal Service, a special government corporation.

When the Postal Service, dedicated to "operating in the black," offered big changes in the postal rates—over a five-year period, the Postal Service suggested, second-class-mail rates for magazines would increase 142 per cent—the magazines saw a real danger to their existence. And they were quite right.

To a large extent the major national magazines had brought this situation onto the shoulders of all the press. In the 1950s and early 1960s, the magazines (*Time, Life, Look, Collier's, Saturday Evening Post, Newsweek, U.S. News & World Report,* and so on) had engaged in vigorous circulation wars to meet television's inroads into their advertising revenues. They had, without question, abused the second-class mailing privilege by selling their magazines at prices far below the cost of production, often almost giving them away. This abuse had brought about huge deficits in the second-class division of the postal system. Nor, in the final analysis, had it saved the weak: by 1973 *Collier's, Saturday Evening Post, Look* and *Life* were all gone.

When the Postal Service announced its plans for drastically higher mailing rates, the magazines were already trying to restore the balance between circulation cost and circulation price and were having difficulty. They had trained the American people to expect cheap prices for magazine subscriptions, and the untraining process in 1972 was not very far along. The publishers of magazines were very worried.

Andrew Heiskell, chairman of the board of Time, Inc., testified before a Senate Subcommittee that the postal increase would raise Time, Inc.'s mailing cost of its magazines (*Time, Life, Fortune, Sports Illustrated*) by $27 million a year at the end of the five years. (Profits before taxes in 1971 were $11 million, which meant the projected increase would wipe out profits altogether and cost the company $16 million more.) And Time, Inc. was relatively well off. Heiskell said that the pretax earnings of *all* American magazines in 1970 were $50 million. Under the proposal of the Postal Service, the increased mailing cost alone would be $130 million more for all magazines. The answer, obviously, was that this would work a tremendous burden on magazines and put many of them out of business.

(Economic arguments had been used before in questions of press freedom. Publishers employed them often over the years, especially with their unions. The attitude of the unions, generally speaking, was that economic problems were the publishers' problems, and many a publication was forced out of business in the 1950s and 1960s because technical progress had not kept up with union demands.)

The postal rate increase would hurt newspapers, too, particularly the country's weekly newspapers. The weekly newspaper press of America, although hurt by the population shifts to the cities, still numbered in the thousands and remained a very important medium of information. True, over two hundred years the function and the relative importance of the weekly had changed. Yet no medium covered the rural and neighborhood countryside with the verve and thoroughness of the weekly newspaper. In 1972 the postal rate increase posed the most serious threat of all to the weeklies: it could raise the mailing costs of the weeklies as much as 500 per cent, and with many weekly papers this might mean the difference between survival and failure.

According to the 1844 principle of operation for the postal service, the government has a special responsibility that goes beyond making money for a government-oriented agency, even in a money-oriented society. But by the 1970s the principle, once believed to be established, had somehow come unravelled and needed to be restated and even rethought.

What would happen with the postal increase was not certain, but in the final analysis it *was* certain that Congress would have to guarantee somehow the freedom of the press, and that if one wanted to call it postal subsidy, then so be it.

The press has lived for two hundred years with postal subsidy, just as have the shipping lines and, more recently, the airlines. The postal subsidy has been a payment by the general public out of general funds, on the principle that freedom of the press was desirable. The public was not wrong in the beginning, and the public was not going to be wrong by insisting on a continuance of this postal policy in the 1970s.

If public insistence is neither strident nor insistent today, then that is one of the problems the moguls of the press have brought on themselves—they have misused the public weal enough, caused a general distrust of the actions and motivations of the press. Now when the press is in trouble because of inflation and bureaucratic zeal, its public champions may, unfortunately, be hard to find.

CHAPTER 8

Radio and Public Affairs

Radio in the first decade of the twentieth century was surrounded by a tangle of technical developments, patent disputes, and intraorganizational squabbles. Government control or censorship was not even of minimal concern, and responsibility to a growing public audience seldom, if ever, crossed the minds of the entrepreneurs of radio. Hundreds of amateurs flooded the airwaves with signals, words, and music. It was all experimental.

Despite this confusion, possibly because of it, Congress recognized a need for control by government. Thus Congress passed the first radio-licensing law in 1912, and President William Howard Taft signed a bill requiring that all radio stations secure broadcast licenses from the Secretary of Commerce and Labor, who would assign the wavelengths and time limits. Immediately after passage of this law, over a thousand of the stations then *existing* were licensed. Many more stations undoubtedly continued without licenses. This was the first time government stepped in to control radio communication. It would not be the last.

Individuals and corporations moved rapidly into the radio business. A number of these entrepreneurs relied upon newspaper connections, although news or information was initially of very minor interest. Broadcasters were in the main projecting music via the airwaves. One of the earliest "newscasts" was a real fiasco. In 1916 Lee De Forest, often called the "father of radio," had a regular schedule of "radio telephone" entertainments. He personally went on the air to announce to his listeners the presidential election returns and erroneously claimed victory for Charles Evans Hughes.

The patent disputes were halted during World War I, and amateurs took a back seat while manufacturing companies produced radio equipment for the government. The U.S. Navy was especially instrumental during the war in pushing many technical developments in radio, and the significance and importance of radio as a new medium of communication was brought to public attention. For example, the Navy had taken over private equipment at New Brunswick, New Jersey, and its station, NFF, could be heard clearly in Europe! Even President Woodrow Wilson recognized the impact radio could have, and early in 1918 he broadcast his Fourteen Points over NFF before he sailed to Europe for the peace conference.

Because the Navy had controlled radio during the war, many persons in government felt that the Navy should control it after the war. (Of course the Navy was the staunchest supporter of this idea.) A bill was introduced in the House of Representatives, and Secretary of the Navy Josephus Daniels testified before Congress that the control of radio in the United States should be given for *all time* to the Navy. This brought discussion. Opponents charged that the move would establish a monopoly. Congressman William S. Green of Massachusetts noted that he did not think it was necessary for "one person to own all the air in order to breathe." The bill was finally tabled by the committee that heard the testimony.

The Navy did not give up easily. Some of its members

next proposed that, if they could not have control, radio should be put "in the hands of one commercial concern and let the government keep out of it." Finally, in the fall of 1919 the Radio Corporation of America was established, and although it was to be a private concern, it also provided for a government representative to present the government's views before the new company's board.

Government seemed willing now to disassociate itself from control of radio, and corporations vied with one another to establish radio empires. The amateurs also continued their experimentation. Transmitters were built in back bedrooms and on campuses. Newspapers set up "radiophones." The Detroit *News,* for example, broadcast the primary election returns in 1920 and, later the same year, the Harding-Cox presidential election returns. All kinds of programs began to be transmitted by radio: musical programs, religious discussions and services, prizefights, and even speeches by public officials, such as Secretary of Commerce Herbert Hoover.

Department stores set up radio divisions, newspapers reported news of coming radio broadcasts. In 1920, station KDKA in Pittsburgh was licensed to offer the first *regular* broadcasting service, and by 1922 more than 500 such stations were operating. These stations set about building studios and searching for talent with which to tantalize a public that was now thoroughly alert to the delights both of radio listening and of assembling sets.

Obviously there was no censorship of any kind, and the stations were free to put out over the air whatever they chose, whether it be a baseball game or a violin solo. The only control was self-censorship by the organized stations. In Newark, New Jersey, station WJZ provided the engineer with an emergency switch with which he could shut off an offending performer and put on a phonograph record. The engineer could do this on his own or on signal from the studio. Taboos included lewd jokes and discussion of birth control.

At this time all commercial stations were on the same wavelength, with the exception of one that was given over to government for such broadcasts as weather and crop reports. Since the Department of Commerce did not allocate time periods, there was often tremendous confusion for the many stations operating on the same meter band. By 1922 even government knew that there had to be some further regulation.

Secretary of Commerce Herbert Hoover called a Washington Radio Conference early in 1922, but even he did not know what regulations were needed, or really what his powers were under the old radio act of 1912. Nothing much was settled at this first radio conference; no legislation came out of it, although most participants agreed that regulation was needed, and a few whispered that Herbert Hoover was harboring the thought of becoming broadcasting czar.

The early twenties could be called the time of the "radio craze"; for everyone, it seemed, wanted to get into the act. Transmitters went up on church buildings; department stores built studios. Among those who started radio stations, were a stockyard, a laundry, a poultry farm, and a marble company. The rush was so great that the Department of Commerce had to make another meter band available, and to do this another class of radio stations was established.

At the same time the radio manufacturing companies were progressing in many different directions; some had patents on one item, others on other items, and some of the companies had mutual agreements, so much so that talk of the "radio trust" was often heard in Congress. Finally, in 1923,

Congress asked the Federal Trade Commission to look into the radio industry to see if there *was* violation of antitrust laws, if monopoly did exist. The same month, March, that the FTC was asked to investigate, the second Washington Radio Conference was convened by Secretary Hoover, who found the chaos in radio "simply intolerable."

This conference supported the belief that Hoover had the right to regulate hours and wavelengths. As a result he reorganized the distribution of the wavelengths according to watt power and areas. Congress saw many bills introduced, including some that advocated various forms of government control, or nationalization, or operation of government broadcasting stations. None of these bills passed.

The burgeoning of the radio industry continued, as more and more stations came into being, and more and more people were interested in radio. There was music and more music. Radio drama appeared—with "clean" plots. News as we know it today was still unheard of. Those newspapers that owned radio stations did not do so to use radio as a medium for news, but rather as a device to promote their newspapers. However, interspersed with the music some stations provided "talks," which were in essence reviews of current events.

One of the most famous radio commentators, H. V. Kaltenborn, first started on radio station WEAF in New York as a lecturer on current events. Kaltenborn had worked for the Brooklyn *Daily Eagle*, and had been giving morning current-event talks in the *Eagle* building. When the *Eagle* was asked to participate in talks on WEAF, Kaltenborn was chosen to present them. Kaltenborn's early experiences on radio are of interest relative to the discussion of radio freedom, for he was one of the first commentators to become involved in controversy over the content of a talk.

The problem was opened up when Kaltenborn, in a radio broadcast, criticized Secretary of State Charles Evans Hughes for his manner of dealing with the Russians. Kaltenborn's criticism started a chain of events that culminated in a demand from Washington, through the American Telephone and Telegraph Company, from which station WEAF leased telephone lines, that Kaltenborn be taken off the air. AT&T admitted freely at the time that they had "constant and complete" cooperation with government agencies, and even indulged in censorship before broadcasting to implement this cooperative policy.

WEAF knuckled under, and Kaltenborn left the station, but he continued broadcasting throughout the country from other stations. When he returned to New York, he broadcast for WOR. Again he was censured, for criticizing the New York City government. But this time the radio station, WOR, which was owned by the Bamberger department store in Newark, New Jersey, backed Kaltenborn and ignored threats by the municipal government to bar WOR personnel from city functions if Kaltenborn was not restrained. Radio, then, had won its first victory in a test of its freedom.

Like many newspapers in the 1920s, radio stations were beginning to be formed into broadcasting chains. When President Calvin Coolidge addressed the opening session of Congress in December 1923 his speech was broadcast by a chain of seven stations, all connected by AT&T cables. By the 1924 election, he would speak to the nation over a network of twenty-six stations!

As broadcasting progressed, advertising, which had been abhorrent to the early promoters of radio, now became an issue. Radio executives wanted profits, but they also wanted to be regarded as respectable, so they kept close control on advertising material—for example, they argued about toothbrushing: was it too personal a matter to be discussed on the air?

In the beginning days of radio, talent had been unpaid, artists of all kinds were delighted just to be heard over the airwaves. But before very long there were wrangles about fees, and stations began to pay the performers.

Many internal problems faced the radio companies, but the greatest problem was brought about by government action. In 1924 the FTC finally completed its study and charged that the big companies (AT&T, RCA, General Electric, Westinhouse, and others) did indeed have a monopoly in the field of broadcasting. The FTC also declared that it would continue its investigations.

Secretary of Commerce Hoover was still busy licensing the growing number of stations and arranging station shifts and power and time changes. Many stations, especially small ones, did not keep to their assigned wavelengths, which were crowded, but sought "free air" on other meters. One such station was operated in Los Angeles by the evangelist Aimee Semple McPherson. When threatened by a Department of Commerce inspector for her dial wanderings, she wired Hoover: "Please order your minions of Satan to leave my station alone."

Some station executives felt that there was indeed one-man control of radio and that Hoover was the czar. But there seemed to be some ground for the government's concern, considering that the companies continued to wheel and deal: WEAF, New York, was sold by AT&T to RCA, and became one of the chief outlets of a new company called the National Broadcasting Company.

By 1927 there were 732 broadcasting stations in the United States, and of these only 100 were network-affiliated. The 732 stations ranged from the dedicated, powerful ones that were making news and getting significant attention to those that were used for publicity purposes, representing stores, hotels, and newspapers. Some were operated by educational institutions; some were run as hobbies.

Congress considered this fantastic growth in broadcasting, and then set about framing a new radio law, which it finally enacted in 1927. The law provided that the United States would maintain control over all channels; stations could use those channels by securing a license, and the license was to be granted according to standards of "public interest, convenience, or necessity." Though government was to control the airwaves, government was not to censor them: the licensing authority would have no "power of censorship over the radio communications or signals transmitted by any radio station" and nothing should be done that would "interfere with the right of free speech by means of radio. . . ." This freedom, however, did not apply to "obscene, indecent or profane language."

And licenses could be revoked if monoply was found to exist.

The most drastic change in the licensing of radio stations was the transfer of the licensing power from the Secretary of Commerce to a five-member independent bipartisan commission that would be set up for the purpose. This commission was to straighten out the radio situation; then, after a year, the licensing would again become the province of the Secretary of Commerce.

Sixty days after approval of the new law, all existing licenses were to be suspended, and the newly created Federal Radio Commission would renew them temporarily until it could make proper reallocations and revisions. By March 1928 the FRC decided that a substantial number of stations would have to show cause why they should not be abolished.

After two weeks of hearings the FRC decided that 81 of the 164 stations questioned could have their licenses renewed.

At the same time that radio was receiving government attention, the new medium of television made its first appearance on an experimental basis. In 1928 General Electric experimentation led to the first television drama, a melodrama called "The Queen's Messenger." Other companies were also perfecting telecasting techniques as well as television equipment.

Expansion of radio broadcasting continued in spite of worsening economic conditions during the Depression that began in 1929. Radio was coming of age, and with its growth of facilities it assumed a greater sense of responsibility. No longer were the airwaves filled with just the old "potted palm" music. Efforts were made to cover the news field and to report significant events. For example, in 1930 when the five-power naval conference was held in London, two American radio newsmen were there covering the events, sending reports back to the United States. Another newscaster, with the Columbia Broadcasting System, arranged with the British Broadcasting Company for various English writers and statesmen to speak to America. One of these, George Bernard Shaw, provoked great outrage when he extolled Russia and chastised the United States. Yet Shaw had spoken freely over the air, he was not cut off, rather CBS gave time for reply to a university churchman who disagreed with Shaw.

Although the networks in the early thirties carried current events talks and news coverage, they still had no system of their own for gathering news. News for broadcast was secured from the newspapers and the wire services. But now there were a number of eminent radio commentators: H. V. Kaltenborn, Lowell Thomas, Boake Carter, Edwin C Hill.

The big problem of broadcasting, however, concerned not

content, but the control and interlocking of the big companies. Many small stations went bankrupt during the Depression, but major companies continued expansion, growth, and mutual agreements with one another that seemed suspiciously like collusion. Finally in 1930 the United States Department of Justice brought an antitrust suit against RCA, General Electric, Westinghouse, and AT&T, the giants of the industry. To avoid an actual trial the companies had to disengage themselves from all their entangling alliances with one another. Not an easy task or a welcome one, but they did so after many meetings and much heated discussion.

In spite of the Depression, or possibly because of it, the networks continued to expand; people seemed to find solace and even joy in radio broadcasts. Owners and operators of stations were delighted to discover how important radio was to the American listeners, many of whom would give up almost anything before they would part with their radio set. President Franklin Roosevelt contributed to the medium's growing importance by inaugurating his "Fireside Chats" over nationwide radio. These were not only informal reports to the people, but exhortations to adopt many of the President's new federal programs.

By this time the advertising agencies had firm control of radio. They did not just write advertising copy or sell time, they actually planned and produced programs and thus controlled program content with little, if any, network supervision. The advertising world feared the Roosevelt reforms, especially those that were proposed by the Food and Drug Administration, for fully half the income of the radio business came from food and drug companies.

Early in Roosevelt's administration the Tugwell bill was proposed to demand precise information about product content. It was designed to bring "freedom from fakes." The broadcasting industry set out to defeat the bill, and while it failed to do so, it did cause the bill to be so emasculated that when it was passed advertising was completely exempt from its provisions.

About one-third of radio time was now sponsored programming in prime listening hours. So through their advertising agencies the sponsors of the programs controlled what the radio audience would hear. This was especially true in the field of news. Few sponsors wanted news programs, and the few that did accept them expected to have control. But this was to change because of the attitude of the newspapers.

Newspapers soon learned that the public—and advertisers —were turning to radio, and they began to fight a war in their own way. They were joined in this by the wire services which had been supplying, without charge, what little news the networks used. Now the Associated Press, the United Press, and the International News Service would only provide some AP-affiliated stations with news bulletins, for a fee, but the service would no longer be available to the networks.

Instead of stifling radio competition to newspapers, this move goaded broadcasters into the action they should have taken long before. They began to assemble their own news-gathering systems.

NBC started with a one-man news bureau: Abe Schechter telephoned around to gather news. Since radio by this time was recognized by both the public and government as an important media of communication, calls from NBC got immediate attention, even while newspaper reporters might be standing in the hallways. Thus Abe Schechter was able to acquire enough news material to fill out Lowell Thomas's program and even provide some for newspaper columnist Walter Winchell, who was also on the air.

Executives at CBS attempted to better NBC—then the

leading network—at news-gathering. CBS set up a complete news organization, and so successful were they that newspapers threatened to boycott the network. It was a war of sorts, and finally a compromise was reached by all parties concerned—a compromise that was really a control of radio direction and content. CBS agreed to drop its news-gathering unit, and NBC agreed not to build one; the networks then established, at their own expense, a Press-Radio bureau that was to make AP, UP, and INS bulletins available to radio. These bulletins were supplied under severe restrictions, however: no item was to exceed thirty words; radio commentators could not use news unless it was over twelve hours old.

This compromise plan was doomed to fail because many radio stations refused to follow the network system and instead secured news from newly formed independent news services. One of the latter, Transradio, became successful enough to survive the turmoil of the fight between the newspapers and the radio networks. Eventually, however, because more and more newspapers were acquiring financial interests in radio, news-gathering was started again.

By the midthirties radio had shown that it was not only commercially successful but also influential. Because of that influence more and more interests wanted to use the medium. With the limited number of wavelengths available, it was obvious government would again have to exert some kind of control. Educators were agitating for channels to be set aside for them, and the commercial broadcasters wanted to continue the status quo. The commercial interests won out, for in the new radio law passed in 1935 the only basic change from the law of 1927 was that telephone and broadcasting were brought under the same jurisdiction, as desired by President Franklin Roosevelt. The Federal Radio Commission was replaced by the Federal Communications Commission, and the new agency was to study the question of channel allocation and report its findings to Congress.

The FCC completed its study and reported that the commercial channels were doing just fine in time allotted for their educational efforts. (Commercial radio had, to be sure, begun several public service programs, such as "America's Town Meeting of the Air.") The pleas of educators for their own channels were ignored.

During this period the sponsors still maintained control of the programs, for the FCC had the power, but not the muscle. Its main weapon was licensing: the issuance of licenses and the renewal/nonrenewal of them. When the new commission took over in 1934, there were 593 broadcasting stations and hundreds of experimental stations and amateur stations in the United States. It is estimated that the FCC had to consider more than 50,000 licenses at that time.

The FCC would renew a license if "public interest, convenience, or necessity" were involved, and the basis for renewal was past performance. It was positively stated that the commission could not censor programs, although the charge of censorship was leveled at the commission a number of times when it revealed its standards for renewal. In essence, the FCC made clear that certain actions would not be looked upon favorably when the station license came up for renewal. For example, it could not forbid liquor advertising, but it did emphasize that a station using such advertising—which children could hear—would indeed have to show that it was acting in the public *interest* when its license came up for renewal. In the light of this, most stations avoided using liquor ads since that was a much simpler course than facing an FCC hearing.

Generally speaking the FCC approved and renewed licenses almost automatically, so really it exercised little power and little control. The sponsor was still the one who dictated broadcast content. The manufacturer of Cream of Wheat sponsored Alexander Woollcott over CBS, and when the firm received complaints from listeners about Woollcott's derogatory remarks concerning Adolf Hitler, it asked Woollcott to refrain from similar comments in the future. Woollcott would not promise to do so, and his series was cancelled. So radio was quite free of external restraints for its broadcast content—except by the *sponsors,* who made the networks richer each year.

The two chief networks CBS and NBC (in reality NBC had two networks: NBC Red and NBC Blue) were now joined by Mutual Broadcasting Company. Competition among all the networks was great. In addition, all radio faced the ultimate threat of television, though that media was still in the experimental stages, and of FM (frequency modulation) broadcasting, which was almost static free. But radio would ride high for some years to come—its power to influence not yet challenged by the new technology.

Radio was used by causists of all kinds to promote points of view, and only sponsor or network displeasure prevented dissemination of all kinds of ideas. However, from the beginning, serious matters took a back seat to the entertainment that radio offered. The airwaves were occupied for the most part by musicians, comedians, soap operas, dramas of crime and of love. And they all brought in money. During the year 1937, the FCC commissioner noted that the networks had taken in over $56 million in time sales, of which over $15 million was passed on to affiliate stations and over $8 million went to advertising agencies as commissions. The commissioner said that the broadcast industry as a whole was making a 350 per cent per year profit on its investment!

However, as the profits grew, there were some small signs that responsibility was growing too. In addition to the "Lone Ranger," and the "Green Hornet," and the "Romance of Helen Trent," there were more serious programs, such as the "Cavalcade of America," good experimental drama by theater groups, and a beginning cognizance of the importance of news coverage in a world where clouds of war were beginning to form over Europe.

Most of the new and rewarding developments occurred in that large spate of time that was unsponsored. H. V. Kaltenborn had been a CBS news analyst for some time, but was seldom sponsored. He had gathered a loyal following, however, because of his constant travel and contact with foreign places and faces. During the Spanish Civil War, he planned to broadcast to America, over shortwave, the actual sounds of war. He made the arrangements, and at the scheduled time was in the thick of the Battle of Irun. Delayed by several sponsored programs, his Battle of Irun finally got on the air. Kaltenborn continued his excursions in the war areas, and made further broadcasts from France. It was an important step forward in showing radio's impact in reporting world news.

By 1937 affairs had become so tense in Europe and American interest in those events had become so apparent that CBS hired Reporter Edward R. Murrow to go to Europe and organize a news-gathering team. When Hitler marched into Austria in 1938, Murrow was in Vienna to broadcast by shortwave the fall of that city. There were other broadcasts from William L. Shirer in London, Pierre Huss in Berlin, Edgar Ansel Mowrer in Paris, Frank Gervasi in Rome, and Robert Trout in New York. Then Hitler began to threaten Czechoslovakia, and the events leading to the Munich crisis in which Czechoslovakia was sacrificed held American audiences spellbound, for day after day shortwave pickups were made from Europe, and Americans heard the voices of Hitler, Mussolini, Chamberlain, Daladier, Beneš, and Masaryk. Kaltenborn was the interpreter of the news for CBS, but now, instead of waiting for sponsored programs to be cleared, the reverse was true: the commercial programs were canceled so that Kaltenborn could be heard.

The success and impact of the Kaltenborn broadcasts were suddenly to thrust the radio commentator into the forefront of radio broadcasting, to be sure in unsponsored time in the beginning, but what a change from the time news bulletins had been interspersed with potted palm music! NBC Red hired Dorothy Thompson as a commentator, NBC Blue got General Hugh S. Johnson; Mutual had Raymond Swing and Quincy Howe. Now, as sponsors began to be attracted to news programs, networks assumed new responsibilities in this era of world turmoil. News became good business.

AM radio continued to grow as a business and was recognized as a powerful medium. It was only the war in Europe that prevented its potential electronic competitors from eroding radio's success and power. When RCA unveiled television in April 1939 at the formal opening of the New York World's Fair, President Roosevelt appeared on the telecast. A mobile unit was now telecasting baseball games, wrestling and boxing matches, and fashion shows. But suddenly a halt was called. Materials to make television sets were needed for war. By May 1940, although twenty-three stations were set up for telecasting in the United States, only six maintained limited programs for the 10,000 sets that had been sold. In 1941 the government took over the shortwave radio stations. Frequency modulation (FM) programming for the public was discontinued and FM broadcasting was reserved for military use only. So AM radio was left with a clear field, for the moment.

Before Japan attacked Pearl Harbor in 1941 the war in Europe caused much furor and discussion in the United States, and much dissension. Some people were isolationist and wanted to stay clear of entanglement in other countries' affairs; some feared that if Hitler won out, world disaster would follow. Many persons and organizations, realizing the power and impact of radio, wanted to make their views known over the air. Executives at the networks were faced with deciding what could or what should be broadcast.

William Paley, head of CBS, decided on a policy of balanced discussions of heated topics and against selling time for the presentation of various viewpoints. Years before the Munich crisis he had said that CBS should not have an editorial page of its own. Now he further insisted that a radio newsman should not propagandize with his own personal views or any other specific views. Thus, he changed the role of the newsbroadcaster. No longer would he be a "commentator"; instead he would become a "news analyst," offering not comment, but analysis.

This new policy was especially hard on Kaltenborn who for years had been freely expressing his own opinions. When he became famous because of his coverage of the Munich crisis, the General Mills company decided to sponsor him and said they would give him complete freedom in his news "selection and in expression on that news." Yet General Mills soon requested Kaltenborn not to discuss the Spanish Civil War. Kaltenborn refused to comply, and General Mills did not renew their sponsorship. The "analyst" role was not congenial to Kaltenborn, and he continued to say what he thought. Eventually he moved to NBC.

But soon all three networks issued a joint statement about broadcasters' coverage of the spreading European conflict: following Paley's lead, they decreed there was to be no personal expression of editorial judgment; the broadcaster was not to try to influence action or opinion of others in any fashion. The FCC agreed in its doctrine of 1941: "the broadcaster cannot be an advocate." Two years before, the National Association of Broadcasters had said the same thing in its code: news broadcasts should not be editorial but should be free of bias, and time should not be sold for presentation of controversial views, except for political broadcasts.

It was easy to see why the industry tried to regulate itself, for it recognized its impact. A *Fortune* poll at the time showed that more people relied on radio for news than on newspapers.

As the tempo of the war in Europe increased so did the numbers of radio newsmen, among them many who would achieve national fame—Eric Severeid, Larry Leseuer, Elmer Davis, many, many others. By the middle of 1940, there were over twenty pickups each day from Europe by the American networks, and Murrow in particular was to be remembered for his coverage of the air war known as the Battle of Britain.

Suddenly, on December 7, 1941, the United States, too, was at war. Now censorship or guidelines could no longer be entrusted to the judgment of network executives. The U.S. government on December 16, 1941, established an office of censorship on a *voluntary* basis—a plan that surprisingly proved to be extremely effective. Broadcasters could submit their radio scripts for review if they wanted to, but it was not obligatory (and few did). Weather news was abandoned, news about troop or ship movements could not be reported. It was urged that ad-lib programs not be presented, for control of them was impossible.

During the war, amateur stations could no longer operate, but the FCC used them to monitor foreign shortwave broadcasts, and this Foreign Broadcast Intelligence Service monitoring proved of great use. The government participated in radio in another way during the war: through the Office of War Information it took over a number of existing shortwave radio stations and established others. Their broadcasting efforts were frankly designed to present "American Propaganda" to foreign countries. The Armed Forces Radio Service also came into being at this time to entertain and inform the troops.

Radio continued to boom during the war. Advertisers flocked to it as an industry both rich and respected. A government survey in 1942 substantiated the respectability and responsibility of radio when the results of its questionnaire were reported. To the question: "Do you have more confidence in the war news on the radio or the war news in newspapers?" 46 per cent of those queried said radio, 18 per cent said newspapers.

As more and more U.S. radio reporters were heard from Europe, there was movement in the opposite direction also. The American Broadcasting Station was created in Europe, and recordings were made by several heads of government, including King Haakon of Norway and General Charles de Gaulle of France, to be broadcast to resistance groups in occupied lands.

There were technical developments in news coverage, too; the correspondents in the field now had wire recorders, which they used during the D-day landings in Europe in 1944. As the Allies fought on, capturing city after city in France and Belgium, the rush was to the radio stations as the means of informing the liberated peoples of the news. Finally in September 1944, Radio Luxembourg, the most powerful station in Europe, became an American voice.

Radio continued to be influential in domestic matters, too, and it was the control of this influence that bothered the FCC. At the beginning of the 1940s more than one-third of all radio stations were owned or controlled by newspapers. In ninety-eight places the *only* radio station was owned by the *only* newspapers. The FCC studied the problem, and finally came up with a report on chain broadcasting and suggestions for diversifying station ownership. Among its recommendations was one that called for NBC to shed one of its two networks. The Supreme Court in 1943 upheld this view and NBC Blue was put on the market. The network was bought by other interests and eventually became the American Broadcasting Company.

CHAPTER 9

Television's Impact

By the time of the Japanese surrender in 1945, plans were underway for the resumption of television set manufacture, and the resumption of manufacture of radio receivers for home use was approved.

The FCC knew that another boom was coming, yet the commissioners worried about the amount of control they had over the burgeoning broadcasting industry. Because the FCC had limited a single owner to six AM stations, owners who controlled more than that number sold or traded some of their stations. The FCC found that in many instances it was not licensing stations, but was merely watching stations change hands, independently of the commission. And too often the FCC had automatically renewed licenses, without first investigating the programming the stations had done in the past, as the FCC had been directed to do back in the 1934 communication hearings.

Now, after the war, the attention of the FCC focused on charges that programming by many stations was deteriorating. The commissioners decided to launch a research program to study the performance of the broadcasting stations. The report of their findings was issued in the spring of 1946. It was entitled *Public Service Responsibility of Broadcast Licensees,* but since its cover was blue, it soon became known as the "blue book."

The emphasis of the fact-finding was not on the networks but on local broadcasting. By analyzing the program content of stations, the FCC discovered excesses in the number of commercials being broadcast, and a failure by stations to produce the glowing programs they promised to do when seeking license renewal.

The blue book set forth standards for licensing renewals: henceforth, the FCC would examine the time devoted to sustaining programs, to local live programs, to discussion of public issues, and would also evaluate the station's resistance—or lack of it—to advertising excesses. (During a typical week in 1944, one station studied in the report was found using 90 per cent of its air time for commercials.)

The furor the blue book caused in the broadcasting industry was astounding. Some media people praised it fulsomely; others damned it as censorship, saying that any FCC decisions based on programming constituted censorship and violated the freedom of speech guarantees in the Communications Act and in the Constitution. By the end of 1946 it was clear that the blue book was a good philosophical treatise, but that it would be ignored by many stations.

Lee De Forest, one of the very first persons to become interested in radio many, many years before, was aghast at the status to which it had fallen and wrote a letter to the National Association of Broadcasters which appeared in the Chicago *Tribune*: "What have you gentlemen done with my child? . . . You have sent him out in the streets in rags of ragtime, tatters of jive and boogie woogie, to collect money from all and sundry for hubba-hubba and audio jitterbug. You have made of him a laughing stock to intelligence. . . ."

Broadcasting has always been full of contradictions, however. At the same time that excessive commercials were being aired and the odd new creature known as the "disk jockey" was making his appearance, Edward R. Murrow was organizing the CBS Documentary Unit which would concern itself with issues of national and international importance. Thus responsibility and irresponsibility went side-by-side in the postwar years of radio.

There were clear signs, though, that the radio boom would be over with the return of television. FM lost its plea for the desired airwaves, which made all prewar FM sets worthless, but television received the spectrum space it wanted. RCA was now talking about television sets by the middle of 1946, and talk became reality when black-and-white sets came on the market that summer. By July the FCC had issued twenty-four new television licenses. In January 1947 the opening session of Congress was televised. More and more applications for television licenses were received by the FCC —but by now the FCC was receiving unsolicited guidance from the FBI.

For this was a time when the country began what later became known as the "McCarthy era." Senator Joseph R. McCarthy was propelled into fame when he accused the United States Department of State of harboring members of the Communist party, who, he said, were shaping State Department policy. Suddenly no one trusted anyone else, and great was the fear of "card-carrying" Communists or Communist sympathizers or those who belonged to Communist-front organizations.

President Harry Truman established a loyalty-security program under which federal employees were checked by loyalty review boards. The Attorney General prepared a list of subversive organizations. The House Committee on Un-American Activities held hearings that were televised.

And it was in this suspicion-and-fear-pervaded atmosphere that the FBI advised the FCC that certain applicants for broadcast licenses were members of the Communist party or were Communist party sympathizers. The FCC sought confirmation of the charges and could find none. Even though the FBI's advice was wholly unsupportable, the feeling in the country against alleged Communists and so-called fellow travelers was so strong that the FCC merely sent FBI Director J. Edgar Hoover a conciliatory letter, stating that it would welcome future advice. Rumors were that McCarthy felt that the FCC itself, as well as some of its licencees, needed purifying.

The witch-hunt in the entertainment area had started with the film industry in Hollywood. Its spread to radio and TV was inevitable—helped along by several organizations, one of which began publishing a weekly newsletter, "Counterattack: The Newsletter of Facts on Communism," in mid-1947. It listed celebrities and actors who engaged in "front" activities, people who attended meetings of organizations that were considered subversive. Those on the list might be "dupes," "innocents," it did not matter—they all "helped Communism." As the fury mounted, the American Legion joined the fray, and people were urged to contact radio and television sponsors who employed entertainers with known "front records." Although the FCC called a halt to issuing of television licenses in 1948—a freeze that lasted until 1952 because of the Korean War—there were still 108 television stations operating, indeed a fertile field for control by pressure groups.

The publishers of "Counterattack" now published "Red Channels: The Report of Communist Influence in Radio and Television," which listed 151 people who were "infiltrating" broadcasting for the purpose of serving the Communist party and the Cominform. "Red Channels" stunned many people in the broadcasting industry, for among the denounced were a number of writers, directors, and performers who were talented and admired. The citations often seemed ridiculous—they included persons who had opposed Hitler and Mussolini, who opposed censorship, or the House Committee on Un-American Activities. Most of the people on the list had been supporters of Franklin Roosevelt's New Deal.

"Red Channels" affected almost everyone who was listed in it; actors could not get jobs; sponsors did not want "controversial" people on programs. Individuals ran campaigns in which they threatened to boycott certain food products if programs used persons listed in "Red Channels." And since supermarket products brought in over 60 per cent of the revenue of the broadcasting industry, the blacklisting became very effective. By 1951 both networks and advertising agencies had set up "security divisions" to check out the loyalty of writers, actors, and directors. Many firms were developing their own private blacklists.

It seemed that there might be a reprieve after Dwight Eisenhower took office as President in 1953, but there was not. When President Eisenhower had to appoint a new member of the FCC, he chose a McCarthy follower. When a second vacancy on the commission occurred, he again appointed an admirer of McCarthy. So the McCarthy investigations continued digging out alleged "Communists" who had "infiltrated" into the State Department. State Department employees were tried and budgets were cut. Among the charges McCarthy made was that in the United States overseas libraries there were some 30,000 books written by "Communists."

The air of suspicion that filled Washington reached far beyond that city. At the networks and agencies the security people continued to consult their blacklists when talent was being hired. New lists were drawn up by a group called

Aware, Inc., which had as its aim war on the "communist conspiracy in the entertainment world."

The coverage of news by television in the early days of the 1950s was superficial and limited. NBC-TV had the "Camel News Caravan," fifteen minutes with John Cameron Swayze, and CBS-TV had fifteen minutes of "Television News with Douglas Edwards." The trouble was that the newscasts concerned matters for which film was available, and much of that film had been shot as coverage of planned events. In this atmosphere one broadcaster came forth who was to be instrumental in causing the eventual decline of McCarthyism and the disgrace of its main advocate, Senator Joseph McCarthy. Edward R. Murrow, remembered for his bravery, his insight, his courage, his calm when reporting World War II from bombed London, now was to show courage in the face of an American ideological enemy.

In November 1951 Edward Murrow and Fred W. Friendly had started "See It Now," a program designed to provide better in-depth coverage of the issues facing the United States. Among these issues was guilt by association that was the apparent divining rod of McCarthyism. In their research for program material Murrow and Friendly came across the case of an army lieutenant in the Air Force Reserve who was asked to resign his commission because his sister and father had been accused by unidentified sources of having radical leanings. The lieutenant refused to resign, and an Air Force board ordered his separation, as a security risk.

The "See It Now" crews went to Michigan and investigated the case, but could get no statement from the Air Force. Murrow and Friendly knew that the program would be one-sided, but they knew the subject—guilt by association —was important, so they decided to air it. CBS executives declined to run a newspaper ad for the forthcoming program, so the producers spent their own money to do so. The public's reception of the program was tremendous. Reaction to McCarthy terrorism had begun.

Next, Murrow and Friendly were asked to film a Civil Liberties meeting. But before this program went on the air, the Secretary of the Air Force announced in a film interview that he had decided the Michigan lieutenant was not a security risk after all and would be retained in the Air Force. It was a victory for freedom and for the "See It Now" producers.

Not all reaction was favorable, though: a number of the CBS-affiliated stations were not pleased and anti-Murrow sentiments were expressed to Alcoa, the program's sponsor. But Murrow and Friendly kept on, and in 1954 their "See It Now" report focused directly on Senator McCarthy's own career. Again CBS refused to promote the two-part program in an ad, so again the producers did. In the first segment, Murrow's comments on the film footage of McCarthy were brief but telling. The second half of the program consisted of a typical McCarthy hearing, during which McCarthy did most of the speaking. In an attempt to be fair, the producers offered the senator a chance to reply to the program, the reply to be paid for by CBS. McCarthy accepted, and in his remarks he spoke of Murrow as "the cleverest of the jackal pack which is always found at the throat of anyone who dares to expose individual communists and traitors."

The "See It Now" television programs focused strong attention on McCarthy's methods. So did the televised proceedings of the McCarthy committee hearings over ABC. McCarthy's argument with the Army that followed in 1954 revealed him to a wide national audience as a bully who vilified his victims by innuendo, smear tactics, and guilt by association. On December 2, 1954—partly, no doubt, in reaction to the televised hearings—the Senate voted 67-22 to censure Senator McCarthy.

But McCarthyism did not die hastily, or easily. The ideas the senator had fostered and the small, but noisy and effective group of his followers continued to contaminate American society. In 1956, two years after the Senate hearings, John Henry Faulk, a WCBS disk jockey and panelist, was elected and took office as vice president of the New York chapter of the American Federation of Television and Radio Artists. The group had been cautious about selecting its officials. Faulk, along with Charles Collingwood, CBS newsman who would be president, had been chosen as "middle of the road." Both had declared themselves as non-Communist. But at the same time they also spoke out against the tactics of such groups as Aware, Inc. Aware was aroused, and even though Faulk had not appeared on any blacklist before, it now issued a bulletin claiming Faulk was connected with various "Communist" activities. Some of the charges were completely false, the others were built on guilt by association. Even so, the sponsors defected and CBC fired Faulk, which made him virtually "unemployable." Faulk raised a suit against his persecutor. He received no financial help from CBS, but CBS News Director Edward R. Murrow sent him a personal check for $7,500 to hire the noted lawyer Louis Nizer. Faulk was vindicated—six years later. He won the suit and a very sizable award for damages. But nowhere in the long proceedings did the network exhibit any basic understanding either of freedom or of media responsibility.

The McCarthy era witch-hunt finally ran its course, but neither freedom nor broadcast industry responsibility was served while it lasted. The McCarthy era, and its disastrous effect on freedom of the airwaves, showed very clearly the responsiveness of the electronic media to hysteria and the inability of these media to withstand financial pressures. It also emphasized the need for continued and strengthened FCC regulation of industry practices.

As television continued its 1950s' boom, such programs as "See It Now" were shoved into the "intellectual ghetto" of Sunday afternoon, pushed to one side in favor of that great income-producer: entertainment. By the middle of the decade, there were more than 500 television stations in the U.S., 85 per cent of all homes (40 million) had television sets, and persons were watching TV an average of five hours a day. Thousands and thousands of sponsors were spending over a billion dollars a year in television. There were the "jackpot" programs, such as the "$64,000 Question." There were hundreds of Hollywood film shows, including many Westerns. Radio was booming, too, with the success of the disk-jockey programs.

What was not booming was noncommercial TV. There were only two dozen of these stations, and they were struggling. National Education Television was kept going by the Ford Foundation. But the clamor for razzmatazz programs in peak hours continued unabated.

Few were the serious voices raised against the average television fare. Senator Estes Kefauver, while studying the increase in juvenile crime, wondered aloud whether television violence was contributing to that crime, but few other such voices were heard. Edward Murrow, whose "See It Now" was finally dropped as too expensive, was distressed by what television had become. But the march tempo of Hollywood-produced television programs just continued to quicken.

In spite of preoccupations with amusement, the networks did manage, from time to time, to initiate or cover events of world significance. CBS invited Nikita Khrushchev to appear on "Face the Nation" from Moscow, and he accepted. Some congressmen were appalled at the network giving time for "propaganda," but most reaction to the program was favorable. Then Vice President Nixon's trip to Moscow in 1959 was telecast by all networks. When Khrushchev came to the United States that fall, some 375 reporters followed him and dozens of TV programs on Khrushchev were produced.

But 1959 did not end well for the broadcasting industry. There were scandals involving the quiz programs and radio "payola" (gifts as bribes paid to disk jockeys). Congressional committees and FCC studies showed that there was a distasteful aura about TV programming. The networks hastened to announce plans for documentaries and projects on serious subjects, but this did not still the clamor for further housecleaning.

There also developed a need for housecleaning in the FCC when, during the hearings about bribes to disk jockeys, it was revealed that FCC Chairman John C. Doerfer had accepted "amenities" and another commissioner had accepted a bribe for his vote on a Florida channel.

Perhaps one of the most disgraceful manipulations of the airwaves concerned the Mutual Broadcasting System, which had been purchased in 1958 by Hal Roach, Jr. Mutual's president, Alexander Guterma, took $750,000 from the Dominican Republic dictator, Rafael Trujillo, to broadcast, for eighteen months, a "monthly minimum of 425 minutes of news and commentary regarding the Dominican Republic." Thus an entire network was "bought"—bribed. The deal fell apart when Guterma became involved in legal problems, and the Dominicans sued to get their money back. But the precedent demonstrated that radio and TV had to be controlled by the FCC, and more stringently than they were.

Though no one would dispute that entertainment, mainly Hollywood films, made the profits for the networks, and thus took up a tremendous percentage of programming time, by the 1960s it was obvious that world events had shaped the growth and improvement of the networks' news divisions. And when news *did* get a portion of the airwaves, it often was spectacular. There was Khrushchev conducting a filmed tour of the U-2 wreckage—to shame the U.S. government, which had lied to the country via a television press conference in which the State Department chief announced there had been no deliberate attempt to violate Soviet air space. There was the abortive summit conference in Paris; Charles de Gaulle, Harold Macmillan, Nikita Khrushchev, and Dwight D. Eisenhower were seen by millions of television viewers throughout the world.

The networks were all now developing their own documentary units, and they announced they would only air news documentaries produced by their own units. This was a blow to the independent producers who felt that the networks were acting monopolistically, which of course they were, while excusing themselves as needing control for "objective, fair and responsible presentation of news developments and public issues."

The news divisions produced the documentaries—and there were some excellent ones produced at this time—but it was the network executives who decided on the scheduling, whether in prime time or not.

Television had grown to be very important in American society; over half the people in the United States depended mainly on television for their news. Yet this news still consisted of early evening fifteen-minute telecasts and a few others.

Television was, of course, important in the election campaign of 1960. During that campaign, the issue of "equal opportunities" for use of air time by the candidates came up and was neatly sidestepped by Congress. Section 315 of the Communications Act said that if one candidate used a station, the station had to give other candidates the same usage. The networks had hoped to have a series of debates between John Kennedy and Richard Nixon, but the question arose: would all other candidates for the Presidency have to be given time? Congress merely suspended section 315 for the 1960 presidential elections. The issue remained undecided, but the congressional action allowed the debates to be televised, and it was estimated that between 60 and 75 million viewers watched and heard them. John F. Kennedy once said after viewing one of his television appearances, that he would not have had a chance for the Presidency in 1960 without "that gadget."

After Kennedy was elected President, he appointed Newton Minow as chairman of the Federal Communications Commission. Here was a man for the broadcasting industry to watch. First of all, Minow favored strengthened noncommercial television. He pointed out to the broadcasters that when television was good, nothing was better, but when television was bad, nothing was worse. He spoke of the "vast wasteland" of television and promised that licenses would not be *automatically* renewed.

Perhaps spurred by Minow's expressed determination to better television and cognizant of the impact of world affairs on the American public, networks began expanding their news divisions, adding to their budgets, scheduling longer news shows (thirty minutes), and providing a more favorable time for specials and documentaries. A Roper poll now showed television rather than newspapers to be the chief source of news for the *majority* of the American people.

The networks became more courageous in the subjects they covered and began including racial discrimination and civil rights. These were not, however, the popular programs that drew immediate sponsorship. For example, NBC-TV found it most difficult to secure sponsors for a three-hour documentary on civil rights in 1963. Sponsors were still very much in control of network programming.

Yet the networks pushed aside the sponsors for four days in November 1963, when commercials were suspended during the detailed, complete coverage of the assassination and funeral of John F. Kennedy. How many television viewers openly wept will never be known, but millions and millions of Americans followed the extraordinary and sad events. And while these were going on, in Dallas another drama was unfolding for the television cameras.

Largely, so it was said, to accommodate the TV camera crews and reporters, Lee Harvey Oswald, who had been arrested and was being held as Kennedy's assassin, was being transferred from the Dallas city jail to the county jail at noon, rather than at midnight the night before, as had been originally scheduled. The result was the live filming of the shooting of Oswald by Jack Ruby. As some commented, if television had not created the atmosphere and pressures upon the police, perhaps Oswald would not have been killed. Certainly he did not get a fair hearing before that, on television, when officers were speaking of "murder" weapons, and of enough evidence to convict him. Spokesmen of the American Civil Liberties Union as well as others of a legal mind, wondered about the quality of justice that television had brought about.

There was much in the decade of the sixties for television to report, but in spite of the special efforts made to cover the news or to study issues in depth, FCC Chairman E. William Henry, who succeeded Newton Minow, referred to television schedules as an "electronic Appalachia." TV and radio were booming, but booming in a flood of commercials and Hollywood's now-popular spy-type TV films.

With the escalation of the Vietnam war by President Lyndon Johnson in 1965 and 1966, some television reporters were distressed at what they claimed was misleading information passed out by government spokesmen about the conditions and situation in Vietnam. Networks had established bureaus in Saigon, and there were literally hordes of television newsmen there. Some reporters felt that the network executives openly favored the government position and did not welcome any coverage that might be disturbing or inflammatory.

The Senate Foreign Relations Committee began hearings on Vietnam. These were televised on CBS and NBC, but CBS refrained from televising testimony given by George Kennan, a strong critic of Vietnam policy. This selectivity on the part of the CBS executives caused Fred Friendly to resign. He wrote in part: "The decision not to carry the hearings makes a mockery of the . . . News division crusade of many years that demands broadest access to congressional debate."

In these years tensions over the Vietnam issue were high everywhere in the country, and they would remain so. Riots, demonstrations, antiwar protests, all provided program meat for television coverage, which late in the 1960s seemed to turn against the war. Commentators, such as Chet Huntley and David Brinkley and especially Walter Cronkite, appeared to be impartial and honest in their evening news. Yet other attitudes were often shown by reporters in the field. Perhaps the country was in too much turmoil for objectivity to be retained in all the productions of the network news divisions.

Programs of the Public Broadcast Laboratory, supported

by the Ford Foundation, reflected much of the country's antiestablishment anger. President Johnson had finally acknowledged the need for development of noncommercial television, and at his urging the Corporation for Public Broadcasting had come into existence, with Frank Pace, Jr., a former Secretary of the Army and former chairman of the board of General Dynamics, as its chairman.

No matter how hard the stepchildren of news and documentaries tried, though, they were always being overshadowed in commercial network programming by the entertainment and were generally shoved to one side by network executives and advertisers and their agencies.

Then tragedies and excitement would occur—the assassination of Martin Luther King, the assassination of Robert Kennedy, the Poor People's March on Washington, the Chicago Democratic convention where heads were cracked and seen by millions of viewers, the landing of American astronauts on the moon—and the news reporters would be in temporary limelight again.

But by 1970, fifty years after radio station KDKA broadcast the Harding-Cox election returns, television and the electronic media generally still had yet to become the social force that they had the potential to become. Television producers had shown that on coverage of events as they occurred —such as the space launches and President Kennedy's funeral—TV could do an astounding job. But when more subtle forces were at work the television producers of public affairs and news were not on such sound ground. And above all, the dollar sign still cast its long shadow over television and its approach to human events.

CHAPTER 10

Problems of
Television News

Television news in the 1970s (and to a lesser degree radio news) suffered from several diseases, or problems, some of them quite curable—in the same sense that all journalism's problems may be curable in America—and some of them deepseated and ingrained in the nature of the electronic media.

One disease, and perhaps the most curable, was characterized by an affliction that may be called *opinionitis,* or *commentatoritis.* It developed out of the show-business "star system" approach to television news, and it threatened the freedom of the electronic media because the show business/newscasting combination cast doubt on the credibility of electronic journalism.

Opinionitis was a relatively new development. In the early years after World War II and all through the fifties most of the prominent radio and television newsmen were graduates of the printed media who had learned their trade in the so-called fourth-estate tradition of objective journalism. One grand exception was Robert Trout. Basically retired in 1972, Trout was almost purely a creature of the airwaves, having been a broadcaster for CBS News almost from the time the network was first formed. Yet there was no more objective, faithful, careful news reader on the air than Robert Trout.

That other great man of CBS News, Edward R. Murrow,

was always careful with his opinions, too, even when he strayed into the show-business aspects of the media with "Person-to-Person." Murrow, throughout his life, maintained the ·fourth-estate kind of detachment that was supposed to characterize journalism.

Many electronic media executives took a somewhat different stance on the news, though. Their approach was stated very succinctly as far back as 1948 by the news editors of ABC in a reply to one of the network's "string" correspondents who had just come out of Spain. (At that time Spain had been cut off from Western Europe for several years. It was impossible even to take a direct train from Madrid to Paris.) On emerging from Spain, the ABC stringer offered the network news of what was going on in Franco's domain. The offer was transmitted to New York, and the ABC news editors' response came back: "We don't want news; we want broadcasts."

That was the approach of the period—not news, but broadcasts, news *shows*. The news shows, though, were played straight. Whatever the shows' weaknesses, the fault was seldom that the man at the microphone or on the camera was trying to direct the ideas of the audience. But if newspapers themselves failed to maintain that old fourth-estate tradition of objectivity, it could hardly be expected to survive in the electronic media, especially considering that the electronic media are really an arm of the entertainment business.

Historically, it wasn't until the entertainment medium of television overwhelmed radio that the networks really discovered the value of news as an entertainment device. Out of that discovery came the twenty-four-hour-news station and the typical news-and-music format of today's radio programming. And out of that discovery, too, came the whole parade of star performers who have made an entertainment show of television newscasting. The people in charge of TV and radio news in the 1960s and on into the seventies fostered the star system by giving "talent" its head and allowing opinionitis to develop.

David Brinkley, Chet Huntley, and Walter Cronkite were the brightest stars in their news era. Each had his own way of projecting an image of believability. In the Huntley-Brinkley combination, Huntley was a little bit of the heavy, but sincere and forthright. Brinkley was the imp with the wry smile and ready quip, who also managed to project a great goodwill for the world and appeared to be sitting in jovial Jovian judgment on the peccadilloes of humankind. Cronkite was the great face, the great voice, the great presence. That all three were able reporters and editors—they had all been newsmen of the printed media before they turned to television—was of relatively little consequence. For the nature of their job called on them to be *performers.*

A television newsman's stock in trade was never reportorial ability, writing ability, or even the ability to project ideas. Instead it was the appearance, the mellifluous voice, and the "sincerity" of the advertising world. The reporters, the writers, the editors were important—and they were all there as part of the huge and talented backstage cast who put the shows together, but were never seen by the audience. The "stars" were the ultimate "product"—as newspapers are the ultimate product—the work of hundreds of unseen hands and minds.

All television and radio news people were, in fact, performers. So recognizing themselves to be and being so recognized professionally, they belonged to the American Federation of Television and Radio Artists, a performers' union. And for news and reviews of their profession they read *Variety*, the show-business bible. A good review in *Variety* was all important, particularly to a special show or documentary.

Neither the union membership nor *Variety*'s critical reviews were able, however, to help the electronic media to produce more objective, straighter, more useful journalism in the 1960s and 1970s. Any improvements in television during that period were purely technological. By and large electronic journalism in 1972 was not as accurate or as believable as it had been ten years earlier.

Time was what television needed. Time was what the strip show (the nightly news show) did not give it, and when the television and radio producers and reporters mixed haste *and* their own opinions, a kind of chaos resulted. An example involved a series of speeches that President Nixon made about the war in Vietnam at the beginning of the seventies. Each of the networks would come on immediately after the President had finished speaking and second-guess him—"analyzing" what he had said. Usually some outside expert was also called in, and he and the network's regular newsmen were very free with their opinions, which often seemed ill-informed or ill-advised. A far better practice would have been to delay the analysis for twenty-four hours, giving the networks time to pull together the points involved and even to do some research. But journalistic zeal, plus the knowledge that the television audience was assembled for the presidential speech, drove the networks to excess after excess. The result was a kind of disaster for freedom of the news media because the believability of television was so drastically lowered.

Opinionitis, the star system, the whole show-biz approach of electronic journalism jeopardized believability and by so doing seriously threatened the freedom of the electronic media in the 1970s. And the men at the top had to take the responsibility for the standards—or lack of standards—that had permitted the system to develop as it had over the years. They would also have to take responsibility for instituting a cure. For TV and radio news would remain show-biz unless the people at the top who controlled network policy decided to change the system.

Another disease that afflicted television journalism—one that was virtually incurable—stemmed from the kind of material that lent itself to television presentation on a daily basis. A "good" news show was almost always controlled by the film to be aired, and the film's newsworthiness depended on its interest factor. This factor had nothing to do with opinionizing. A television-news producer could never forget the intensely competitive nature of network news shows, and the need to put on the best "show" was paramount. A filmed interview with President Nixon discussing devaluation of the dollar could never compete with action films of the Vietnam war, particularly if the film showed heavy destruction and killing. That is simply the way it was—the worst news usually made the best film, and consequently, even more than the newspapers, television was the slave to human disaster.

Yet another television news problem was the unwieldy nature of the mechanical forces needed to do the job. A print-medium reporter could go out with a pad of paper and a pencil—or even a good memory—observe, return, and write his story. A radio reporter could go out with the same implements, assisted in rendering verisimilitude by a tape recorder. But to do his job, a television correspondent had to have a cameraman, a sound man, and himself on camera. The whole took time and trouble to set up, and it was a constant tribute to the tenacity and ability of the men involved that they did as well as they did in presenting news. But again, the kind of news they could present, overwhelming sometimes in its impact on the TV screen, was limited by available filming subjects. A correspondent simply could not interview the non-English-speaking citizen of a foreign country, no matter how well the correspondent might speak the language. Ed Murrow had experimented with simultaneous translation in his last years at CBS, but he had at least a week in which to work on his special shows, and even so the technique did not prove very successful with audiences.

Where television shone in the 1970s was in its ability to give with unmistakable power a clarifying picture and word view of a situation. Sometimes these views were given in half-hour, hour, or even longer documentary programs. Sometimes they were accomplished in eight- or ten-minute vignettes. The best shows on television, the most useful, were the public affairs shows that focused on public figures for half-hour periods. Americans learned more, for example, about the intransigeance of the North Vietnamese in the CBS "Face the Nation" interview with Hanoi diplomat Xuan Thuy than they had learned in hundreds of reports on the Paris peace conferences. The dreadful impact of sustained economic depression on the people of Seattle was shown graphically on another program.

The best practitioners of electronic journalism were those who were most aware of its serious limitations. Radio and television journalism by its very nature is a headline service —a whole day of electronic news broadcasts would not produce the content of a single copy of one of the major American newspapers. Yet many millions of Americans relied on television journalism by its very nature is a hedline service 1970s. Since there is no really national newspaper in the United States, the responsibility of the electronic news media is far greater today than that of the printed media. Serious-minded broadcasting executives and newscasters were aware of these facts in the 1970s, but they were not coping very well with them. Nor did the direction of television news coverage augur well for the freedom of the news media in the future.

CHAPTER 11

The Electronic Media and Bias

A report in the Summer 1972 *Public Opinion Quarterly* noted that network news coverage of the Vietnam war was not biased. The report was written by a Yale University student and was based on his research study of network news coverage in 1969 and 1970. His findings were good news for the networks. They did not agree, however, with an extensive study of network bias made by Edith Efron and reported in her book, *The News Twisters*, published in 1971.

The issue of news-media bias had to do with opinion versus fact and how American thinking, beginning in the 1960s, had grown to accept opinion for fact in the mistaken assumption that, because the television journalist with a sincere, authoritarian delivery said something, that something was true. Television was largely responsible for this change in American response, for, as pointed out in the preceding chapter, many television journalists suffer from opinionitis. They seemed to believe that they could not report news without letting the world know what they personally thought or how they personally felt about what they were reporting.

It is not the purpose of this book to engage in colloquy on the two schools of journalism. It is enough to say that there *are* two schools: the objective and the subjective, and that until the 1960s the objective school was regarded as the valid school. Practicing journalists believed that truth could be

[133]

sought and achieved by those who opened their minds and looked and were careful to remind themselves of the holy grail of objectivity. Since that time, Brinkley and other news-media people have denied that objectivity is possible and have suggested that all that can be achieved is fairness, matching up of different opinions as well as possible. (In the Efron book, NBC Newsman David Brinkley is quoted as stating: "News is what I say it is. It's something worth knowing by my standards.") Thus we see evidence now of a new kind of journalism in which young people come to the field, not to learn, but to evangelize.

Whether minds are made up and changed by this kind of reporting is still not clear. What seems reasonably certain, though, is that when opinion is injected into news reporting, whether in the printed or the electronic media, the report is bound to be weighted one way or another. Pure reporting can only be achieved when the reporter honestly tries to divest himself or herself of any preconceptions on a given subject, and then reports the facts and only the facts.

Bias is certainly not unknown to the communications media. There have been biased newspapers from Horace Greeley's New York *Tribune* and Colonel McCormick's Chicago *Tribune* to Eugene Pulliam's (Indiana, Arizona) chain of newspapers today. But readers of biased newspapers quickly came to realize the bias and to adjust their thinking for it.

Even in the 1970s the majority of U.S. newspaper publishers are Republican in outlook, and many newspapers have a Republican bias. Some publishers try to divorce editorial bias from the news coverage and maintain that they can achieve objectivity. They may be right, for the majority of reporters have their own personal bias, and it's likely to be liberal or social democratic.

Bias is a different matter in broadcast journalism. The politics of the Stantons, the Paleys, the Sarnoffs, and the other owner-executives of radio and television are not at issue (in fact their politics are virtually unknown) and the managers of news, the divisional presidents and vice presidents, are shadowy figures. Thus the only reality of radio and television is what the listener and the viewer hears and sees. Every time the correspondent or newsman appears, he represents the whole entity.

In the modern newspaper, the reader can usually select on the editorial pages comments from conservative and liberal columnists, and by reading both the person can at least draw his own conclusions. But the total daily output of any network or station cannot possibly be heard or seen by everyone. So every time a citizen turns on radio or television, what comes out of the box represents the whole. That's why objectivity is even more important in radio and television news coverage than it is in the press. It is also why the so-called fairness doctrine is no substitute for objective reporting.

The fairness doctrine requires that all sides in a public issue be given coverage. The broadcasters fought hard not to be bound by the doctrine, contending that it was an abridgment of their freedom of speech under the First Amendment. But the U.S. Supreme Court upheld the principle of the fairness doctrine in 1969.

Yet the fairness doctrine is not a solution to the problem of bias, which may be the single greatest threat to the freedom of the broadcasting industry. When the public is sufficiently outraged by the bias of television and radio reporting, the present Federal Communications Commission will be strengthened—or it may well be replaced by a new and ultrastrong government agency. For a truism of any society is that the public will eventually call for stringent controls to curb what it believes are excesses.

Another important reason for a return to objectivity and extreme care in radio and television reporting is related to the relative impermanence of the product: the broadcast. A broadcast exists only for the length of time it is on the air. Once a radio or TV program is aired, whether it is heard or viewed, that's it. For all practical purposes it's gone for good, and so is the audience, generally. A newspaper, on the other hand, is a relatively permanent entity, and its audience is usually the same group of readers, day in and day out. If a newspaper errs, it can print a correction or a retraction in the same position the next day, with almost perfect assurance that the people who read the original story will spot the correction. If careless reporting on television or radio creates error or, worse, libel, it is practically impossible to correct the error or withdraw the libelous statement. A correction or a retraction can be broadcast, but it is of little if any value if there is virtually no assurance of catching up with the same audience that viewed or heard the original program. Thus there is need for management of the station or network to exercise control so that bias does not *get* on the airwaves in the first place.

A specific program area in which bias may occur is the interview. It is admittedly a most difficult area to control, because so much depends upon the choice of interviewees. The interview itself is legitimate, objective journalism (when decently conducted), but the bias may still be there in the way the questions are put and in the answers elicited.

Edith Efron documents considerable bias in this area during the television coverage of the 1968 political campaign. Democrats interviewed on the subject of Richard Nixon usually tended to become personal, sometimes vicious. According to Ms. Efron's book, in the election of 1968 all three networks tried to defeat Richard Nixon for the Presidency by exhibiting bias, by portraying Hubert Humphrey as a "good guy" and Richard Nixon as a "bad guy."

Another kind of network bias that occurred in the late 1960s and into the 1970s was not personal but institutional: a bias for black militants, radical students, and other admitted enemies of the status quo. According to Edith Efron, "pro-black militant opinion greatly exceeds opinion critical of black militants." She further charges that all three networks cast conservatives as racists, as well.

The technical opportunities of television for a good story can lead to bias, too. A House of Representatives investigating group found that the networks in their coverage of the 1968 Democratic convention in Chicago had deliberately sought out people who opposed the conduct of the convention and Mayor Richard Daley's administration of Chicago and had withheld information that would have been derogatory to the demonstrators. Nor did they speak up, reporters or commentators, about the provocations of the demonstrators—their abusive language, their use of garbage, even excreta—against the police, obviously aimed at provoking a strong response. It was reported that camera crews even faked events, and the example was given of a girl who came forward to National Guard troops, wearing a bandage on her forehead, and on cue from the TV cameraman shouted, "Don't hit me!"

Television news crews have also been accused of telling demonstrators that they could use the media if they would pay the price: performing. Many demonstrators were glad to do just that. Consequently, during various radical and youth demonstrations the public viewed scenes that suggested the whole country was seething with revolutionary intent.

Dr. S. I. Hayakawa, former president of San Francisco

State College, testified before Congress that he believed television was one of the great negative forces of the San Francisco State disturbances of the late 1960s. Lester Markel, student of publicity and policy, had stated his belief that the deliberate misuse of television film should be outlawed—a very serious statement, because of the restrictions on freedom of the media that such outlawing would require.

Before beginning his administration, President Nixon decided that the only way he could sidestep the problem of bias and get fair representation of his views in the nation's press, printed and electronic, was to go over the heads of the owners and reporters, directly to the people. (Franklin D. Roosevelt, a Democrat, had made the same decision when he became President years earlier. He took to the radio with his "Fireside Chats" to carry his views to the American people.) Nixon realized, as had President John Kennedy when he decided to launch the President's live press conference over national television, that with all its deficiencies, the medium of television was the most potent in the land, quite dwarfing the press. He started telecasting early in his administration by introducing his cabinet to the American people via national television on December 11, 1968.

The trials of the Nixon administration in dealing with the press are documented, from the Nixon viewpoint, in James Keogh's *President Nixon and the Press*. What is to be learned from that book about news-media bias is that network bias is more of a problem than newspaper bias. Network bias is more easily seen because television is larger than life.

In the 1970s Nixon stopped having presidential press conferences, and the news media complained that his refusal to hold them threatened freedom of information. But information was seldom forthcoming in the press conferences, and Keogh charges that the basic purpose of the press conference, to inform the people, had been subverted by the newsmen themselves. If freedom suffered, and there is reason to believe it did, the news people had no one to blame but themselves, according to Keogh's findings.

Whether television and radio bias is accidental or whether it is planned at high levels was another of Edith Efron's inquiries. Her answer is that it is more accidental than planned. In other words, there was no conspiracy of the television newsmen to achieve an end—rather all the things that go into television journalism and radio journalism added up to the abuses. There was a dichotomy, and Edith Efron documented it neatly. She noted that while in 1970 Julian Goodman (who was then president of NBC) said that television only reported the news and did not make it, NBC's star newsman, David Brinkley, was saying that news was what he himself said it was; that while Goodman told an audience of broadcasters that television was not a political instrument or a social theory but a means of communication, NBC's star newsman, Chet Huntley told the Radio and Television Society that news was social and political criticism.

The people who run television, the executive-owners, are generally interested in news only because news and public-affairs broadcasting give them the license to conduct their real business, which is entertainment. Consequently, the television and radio network news operations have been allowed almost total freedom of editorial responsibility, but without direction. It seems doubtful that the divergencies of public and industry approaches to public affairs can ever be successfully reconciled, for while public affairs is the prime consideration of the Federal Communications Commission in licensing stations, it is usually the last consideration of the network people themselves.

Late in 1972 Clay Whitehead, one of Nixon's main media advisors, suggested licensing legislation that would force television stations to balance "the ideological plugola" of network news shows. Some stations did that already. Others scoffed at the idea. It was possible that legislation of this kind would be introduced—most improbable that it would ever pass Congress. Printed and electronic media immediately raised voice in protest, which was to be expected. Congress was listening, a 93rd Congress that was very much aware of the infringements on freedom by the executive arm of the government in recent years.

Why, one might ask, did all this seem so important in the 1970s? The answer is that in the 1960s and 1970s Americans became aware for the first time that television was *the* most important factor in the communication between the governors and the governed. Television coverage of political conventions and political activities gave them visibility nationwide in a way that the printed media had not been able to do in nearly two hundred years, and never could do.

Bias in a newspaper, even so great a paper as *The New York Times,* could affect only relatively few people. And bias, by and large, tended to cancel itself out in the printed media because of the relatively small circle of the printed media's influence. But bias in national television and radio could influence a whole nation. It could be deadly. This much was known. The way to eliminate or at least reduce it was another matter.

CHAPTER 12

The Freedom of Television

The question of television bias and television freedom became a matter of public debate between Vice President Spiro Agnew and the television press following President Nixon's November 3, 1969, address on Vietnam via national television. Some commentators took exception to the President's billing the speech as important, and Vice President Agnew took exception to the commentators' and reporters' exception. The great debate went on into the seventies, and the demands and threats that it spawned finally led to a series of investigations. Principal among these was the study of freedom of the media by Senator Sam J. Ervin, Jr., chairman of the Subcommittee on Constitutional Rights.

Early in 1972, Chet Casselman, president of the Radio and Television News Directors Association, appeared before Senator Ervin to testify and to give the point of view of his group. He was concerned, as were many others, whether the First Amendment principles of freedom of the press should apply without restriction to the electronic media. He favored the resolution then in the House of Representatives that would make the provisions of the First Amendment to the Constitution apply to these media.

Casselman believed that, if television and radio had existed when the Constitution was drafted, the First Amendment would specifically have included them. He suggested that freedom of the airwaves for broadcasters was synonymous with "freedom of the people." He also noted that eighteen states had shield laws protecting the newsmen's right to refuse to disclose their sources of information. He felt that broadcasters and the printed media should have unlimited freedom. "We believe the answer to the imperfections of journalism is not government supervision," he said, "but the exercise of a higher degree of self-disciplined professionalism by journalists and their publishers—print and broadcast alike."

Could this be attained? The practitioners thought so. The president of CBS, Dr. Stanton, testifying before the Ervin subcommittee, said that when the Founding Fathers guaranteed freedom of the press, "their point . . . was not to protect any specific medium but to assure forever the right of the people to the full and free interchange of information and opinion—and to put that right beyond the power of government to inhibit or hamper."

Stanton held that the roles of broadcast and print media were identical: to provide the public with news and information and to stimulate public inquiry and criticism by themselves inquiring and being critical. "In view of the essential purposes shared by the broadcast and press media, their dissimilarities pale into total insignificance," he said.

Dr. Stanton presented examples of past attempts by the FCC to inhibit broadcast freedom. He said that on one occasion the FCC scrutinized twenty-eight pages of correspondence over a five-month period before deciding that CBS's presentation of a nine-minute feature on bullfighting did not constitute a public question and did not justify a request from an animal lovers' group for equal time. "This type of detailed examination by a government body is wholly incompatible with effective broadcast treatment of public issues," Stanton said.

He brought up the matter of the fairness doctrine and cited the case of the Miami station that the FCC found had violated the fairness doctrine in a discussion of the casino gambling issue. The FCC had actually counted the words said on each side, and then decided the station should have presented more pro-gambling material.

He also discussed CBS's attempt to exercise the fairness doctrine in behalf of the opposition (Democratic) party. Since the early days of radio, the President of the United States has occupied a special position in being able to speak to the American people at any time on matters he felt were of national importance. In the opinion of the management of CBS, that approach was no longer correct. Their view was that the opposition party should have equal time for reply. In July 1970 CBS undertook to give the opposition party an opportunity for a reply by making time available to the Democrats for the purpose. The Democrats made their broadcast, and then the Republican national committee complained to the FCC. The commission held that the Republicans were now entitled to reply to the Democrats. CBS called that a reply to a reply. The matter was still in the courts in 1972, having reached the Federal Court of Appeals.

Speaking for the industry, Dr. Stanton had other complaints about the FCC. Some stations wanted to exclude all advertisements, paid announcements, on public issues, on the basis that if there were several points of view involved, in fairness the stations and networks would have to sell time to all concerned, thus eliminating their total control of the time they were on the air. "This constitutes a real threat to freedom of the press," said Dr. Stanton, "because it empowers a government agency to decide what issues a journalist must cover—whether or not, as a matter of substance, they meet journalistic standards of relevance and urgency."

Walter Cronkite, the CBS star newsman, noted in the hearings that a handful of men had the "awesome power" of determining what should go on the brief (half hour) nightly news broadcasts of the three networks each day. He believed there was no alternative to this—disregarding the personalities involved—and that the men and women who did this work tried to be fair.

Cronkite saw some limitations on the general freedom of the press and broadcasting. One was the nature of advertising; the media do not unnecessarily offend advertisers, and thus advertisers by their very existence exert a kind of control. Another limitation was profit-making. The owners of the media are likely to be members of the elite, said Cronkite. Other limitations were: the courage—or lack of it —of the men of the media; the limitations imposed by government on access to documents and news sources; the court rulings that forced reporters to reveal their sources. (Some of these issues concerned all journalism and will be discussed in Chapter 14, The News Media and the Government.)

Several of Cronkite's worries focused on the specific problems of broadcast journalism. He referred to an NBC case in 1942 that established the present position of broadcast journalism. At that time the U.S. Supreme Court opinion stated:

Freedom of utterance is abridged to any who wish to use the limited facilities of radio. Unlike other modes of expression, radio inherently is not available to all. That is its unique characteristic and that is why unlike other modes of expression, it is subject to government regulation.

More recent was the famous case, called the Red Lion Decision, of 1969, in which the Supreme Court held that "where there are substantially more individuals who want to broadcast than there are frequencies to allocate, it is idle to posit an unabridgeable First Amendment right to broadcast comparable to the right of every individual to speak, write, or publish."

Cronkite quoted Judge Burger, in a case before he became Chief Justice of the U.S. Supreme Court:

A broadcaster has much in common with a newspaper publisher, but he is not in the same category in terms of public obligations imposed by law. A broadcaster seeks and is granted the free exclusive use of a limited and valuable part of the public domain; when he accepts that franchise, it is burdened by enforceable public obligations. A newspaper can be operated at the whim or caprice of its owners; a broadcast station cannot. After nearly five decades of operation, the broadcast industry does not seem to have grasped the simple fact that a broadcast license is a public trust, subject to termination for breach of duty."

Cronkite said that "stripped of this constitutional protection" broadcast news "stands naked" in the face of its enemies. He brought up a celebrated case, that of the "Selling of the Pentagon"—a documentary telecast prepared and aired by CBS News.

"The Selling of the Pentagon" was put together by an experienced television producer and crew. Its purpose was to expose the methods by which the public affairs sections of the military establishment secure the consent of governors and governed to the will of the military. The telecast was aired in 1971 and caused immediate furor in Washington, D.C. Several officials claimed they were misquoted or quoted out of context. A congressional committee demanded that CBS produce the "out-takes"—that is, the film that was shot and then edited for the broadcast, and especially those parts not used. CBS refused. The congressional investigators tried to force Dr. Stanton to do so through a contempt citation.

The investigation revealed that in editing the film CBS had taken answers to some questions and used them as responses to other questions. Dr. Stanton defended this practice. "The Selling of the Pentagon" was a celebrated affair, for it proved the worst of both sides, government investigators and the broadcasters, in the struggle for fairness and freedom. While the vote to cite Dr. Stanton for contempt was negative and most members of the House of Representatives held for the CBS official, there was still a large body of feeling that broadcast journalism was going too far in its manipulation of the public weal and needed new controls.

As for the charge that broadcasting was a monopoly, Cronkite and others held that this was no longer so in the 1970s. There were unused channels in various cities and areas (largely FM and UHF, the less desirable radio and television channels). But in 1972 there were 6,976 radio stations, 892 television stations, and only 1,766 daily newspapers. The monopoly, said Cronkite, was a newspaper monopoly in the last half of the twentieth century, not a broadcast monopoly. Most cities had more television stations than daily newspapers.

What the broadcasters wanted in 1972 was some kind of legislation to assure them full exercise of the rights of the First Amendment. This would include elimination of the fairness doctrine provision of equal time for all points of view on public issues and, ultimately, elimination of all controls on broadcasting.

In the Ervin subcommittee hearings, FCC Chairman Dean Burch testified about the actual regulations that cover broadcasting. Coverage is not through the networks, except as they *own* broadcasting stations. FCC control is conducted, as it has always been, through the licensing of stations. Burch said that the licensing procedure is still necessary, but contrary to the claims of the broadcasters, he asserted that the protections of the First Amendment *did apply* to broadcast journalism. The Supreme Court had so stated, a section of the Communications Act so provided.

To the broadcasters' argument that there were more broadcasting stations than newspapers, Chairman Burch stated: "This is true. But no one will stop you from putting out a newspaper. Only one person can operate on Channel 4 here in Washington, and all others will be prevented from doing so."

Although there are places for thirteen channels on the VHF dial of every television set, thirteen channels cannot operate anywhere in the United States because of interference with other channels in nearby areas. True, on a Washington dial Channel 2 is reserved for a Baltimore station. It may not come in very well on Washington sets, but it would interfere with a Washington station's operations on the same channel.

The Burch statement also indicated a fundamental difference in approach between broadcasters and newspapers. By its very nature, a newspaper is primarily an organ of communication, transmitting information and comment. The primary purpose of the radio and television station has always been entertainment, and as noted earlier, even the news divisions of broadcasting have suffered from a show-biz complex over the years. Yet, from the public point of view, the primary obligation of the broadcaster is to devote a reasonable amount of time to informing the public on controversial issues.

The words "reasonable time" have never meant the same thing to broadcasters and newspaper publishers. A newspaper that devoted less than 30 per cent of its content to news and public matters (other than advertisements and entertainment) would be in trouble with its readers. A television station that devoted *as much as* 30 per cent of its content to public affairs would be most unusual.

Only recently, under the Nixon administration, has the FCC really been regarded as a threat by the powerful men of broadcasting. Because of the running quarrel between this administration and the broadcasting industry, the FCC paid closer attention to the fairness doctrine and its applications, with an indication that it might seek more stringent standards. For instance, the commission showed a new concern lest there be undue concentration of ownership of radio and television stations. It was conceivable, if there were no restraints, that the networks might acquire control of most of the important local stations. The commission also took steps to encourage local programming by restricting the amount of network programming a station could air. And finally, in the cigarette controversy, the FCC held that stations that advertised cigarettes must also carry the Surgeon General's warning that they could be dangerous. (That ruling persuaded tobacco advertisers that their advertising might easily boomerang, and they chose to cut it out altogether.)

FCC Commissioner Nicholas Johnson, who represented the Democratic views of the FCC, as opposed to Chairman Burch's Republican views, agreed with Burch on the need for continuing control of broadcasting in the public interest. Johnson pointed out in the Ervin hearings that the FCC had consistently refused to enter disputes where the networks were accused of bias and distortion of news and documentaries. He noted that the basic force controlling the broadcast industry was narrow self-interest, and that this posed the most serious problem the industry faced.

"No, it is not the FCC or the Fairness Doctrine that stands in the way of the broadcasters' first amendment freedoms as a trustee for the public," said Commissioner Johnson. "It is the broadcaster himself who censors—censors in the name of saving money, censors in the name of currying favor with advertisers, politicians, or others whose predilections he would rather not offend."

But one special problem of broadcasting freedom did remain—and Johnson made a point of it: this was the imbalance that had grown up that gave the President of the United States such heavy access to radio and television, without giving Congress the same access. Over the years Congress had surrendered much of its power to the executive branch of government. In the 1970s Congress wanted to take some of that power back, but was experiencing great difficulty doing so. Whereas the President could command a nationwide audience, on request, to discuss matters he believed were of national importance, no spokesman for Congress could do the same. The situation obtained, no matter which party was in power—and always redounded to the advantage of the party in control of the White House at the moment.

This problem required serious examination if each branch of government were to have equal use of the media. But the special pleading of the broadcast industry that it be freed of any and all controls placed on it seemed to be of small advantage to anyone except the broadcasters.

CHAPTER 13

Public Television

One sign of healthy ferment within the communications industry in the 1970s was the bigger role projected for public television. The reason for the new interest in public television was simple: it was apparent everywhere in America that commercial television was falling down badly on its public performance.

The main difficulty facing public television was financing. Grants from private foundations and voluntary contributions from viewers were not enough to support public television's ambitious new programming plans. Public TV was forced more and more to turn to the federal government for funds. According to Elie Abel, dean of the Columbia School of Journalism, the problem was "to find some way to make it secure in its financing and also to make it secure against government control of the contents of what is broadcast."

But public TV had another big problem: how to keep from aping Big Brother—commercial TV. This question was spotlighted when public TV got into trouble in 1972 by hiring Sander Vanocur away from NBC at a salary of about $75,000 a year. That was a TV newsman's salary, not a government employee's salary, and it was a bad precedent. Comparison was inevitable between public TV and "Voice of America," a government radio operation that was broadcast abroad. The "Voice" disk jockeys and others who reached millions of listeners were paid by government standards, not by commercial radio standards. Public TV had to learn that producers, writers, and commentators may have reasons over and above income or profit for wanting to work in noncommercial television. Government could not be expected to foot big bills like the Vanocur salary without a reaction. It was wrong to expect otherwise and by the end of the year Vanocur was out of a job.

Idealists could point to Britain and West Germany for the best in public broadcast systems, and, oddly enough, to Japan, which was not usually considered in this light. Broadcasting in these countries was funded by government, and yet a remarkable independence and originality existed. Indeed, the BBC was legendary in radio and then in television for excellent programming, and many of its finest efforts were seen in America ("The Forsyte Saga"; the super-study, "Civilisation"; the stirring "Six Wives of Henry VIII").

In Britain and Germany the financial support of public television came from license fees, collected from owners of sets. In Germany, the set-owner paid $8.00 a year for public television. In Britain the set-owner paid $15.60 for black-and-white television, another $15.00 for color, and $3.25 for radio. Each year in Britain, BBC television and radio collected about $250 million from the general public.

Here in the U.S., contributions from the public were frequently sought by noncommercial stations, but public TV was looking to the federal government for badly needed additional funding. In 1972 Richard Nixon's administration proposed that Congress provide $45 million for one year to fund the Corporation for Public Broadcasting. Any further appropriations were left up in the air. It was a terrible plan, for like any other continuing program, to leave it to the political whim of Congress was to court disaster. Public television would have to be politically responsive, and immediately so. It would have to be careful not to tread on either Democratic or Republican toes. Starting thus, it would inevitably run scared.

Critics of the plan called for long-term financing. But even a dedicated tax or earmarked money over a long period of time, as suggested by the Carnegie Commission, could not do the job. For no U.S. Congress could commit another U.S. Congress to a future course.

Public television would be much better off if it were self-supporting—and there were ways this could be achieved. What was needed was independence, a separate corporation, and user payment, perhaps modeled on the various European payment plans. Congress could not touch such a corporation except to disband it or in some other way regulate it— but in a manner that would be known to every citizen of the United States and that would avoid undue pressures on the producers, the public television network, and the stations.

Meanwhile, in 1972 the fate of public television still rested with Congress. That body debated long and loud whether public television should consider public problems. It also debated whether money should be given to local stations for programming, or whether more money should go to the network. The answer was both.

Over the years since public television began, it has proved its ability to do certain things better than commercial television. This was not inherently true—there was no secret, no mystique involved in public broadcasting. But the public broadcaster knew at the outset that he had to be factual, he had to be fair, and that if opinions were to be aired, they must be labelled as such.

The best illustration of the capabilities of public television came in the Public Broadcasting Laboratory experiments, starting in the 1960s. More recently PBL has tried out some interesting new program ideas. For example, in the political conventions of 1972, CBS and NBC's coverage, as usual, included many vignettes and flashes of activity both inside and outside the conventions themselves. ABC, the third network, did not really cover the conventions in toto, but confined itself to heavily edited summaries, presented once or twice a day. PBL set out to actually show what went on at the convention, without cutting away from what the commercial producers might consider to be the dullest parts. Thus, for the first time, the television viewer could get a real idea of the content of a convention, without interjections by the television news stars or breaks for commercials.

Public broadcasting need not play for ratings, so "in-depth" reporting jobs can be done, and are being done in many programs on public issues. There is no reason that commercial television could not do the same, but would it? Experience dictates the answer: No.

As public consciousness of the limitations of the profit system in commercial radio and television grows, so no doubt will the pressure for an independent, responsible, and strong public television system in the United States.

CHAPTER 14

The News Media and the Government

During the 1960s and 1970s United States society discovered
that there was a large "credibility gap" operating in its daily
life—an apparent disparity between what was being uttered
and what actually had happened in the nation.

Things might be said by people in government that were
denied by subsequent government actions; or there might be
cover-up of information to avoid confronting the populace
with the truth. And things might be reported by the news
media that swung far, far wide of reality. Was all this a phenomenon blown in on the wind to further confound an already troubled people? Or was it deliberate, a machination
of government, of the media, or of both?

Whatever the answer, something was required to relieve
the tensions that were being created in everyone. But what?
Did the conditions call for a tightening of public control of
the news media, perhaps curtailment of the basic freedoms
assumed to be guaranteed under the First Amendment of the
Constitution? Or did the conditions demand an opening up
by government to provide better visibility of its operations?
Or again, was a little, perhaps a great deal, of both the required remedy?

Perhaps the answer can be found in the developments that
led to this credibility gap.

For years, of course, the nation's political figures of all colorations had accused one another of telling lies. The left wing had accused the government of lies, so had the right, and the Democrats were no more immune than were the Republicans to such charges. But in the 1950s certain U.S. actions outside the country—in South America, particularly in Venezuela—brought charges that the United States government had been lying to the people. Then, in 1960, during President Dwight D. Eisenhower's administration, an American spy plane, the U-2, was shot down over the Soviet Union, and U.S. citizens were rocked by another lie. At first, not knowing what evidence the Russians had, President Eisenhower denied that such spy planes even existed. When he was caught in the lie, the whole foundation of presidential and government honesty with the people crumbled. It had not recovered by the 1970s.

Yet it was President Eisenhower who had initiated innovations that he hoped would improve press coverage of government activities and so better inform the people. He was the first President to allow direct quotations of the President in the press and the first to allow taping of press conferences for broadcast on radio and television.

Perhaps these changes should not have been made. For over the next three administrations they helped to strengthen the adversary system between President and reporters. Knowing that whatever he said would most certainly be used against him by his enemies if they could, a President had to become extremely cautious and apparently "slippery" in his dealings with the news media. There could no longer be any "off-the-record" explanations, for everything was for the record. The press that had once occupied a favored "inside" position began to lose that position. The result was frustration of reporters and increased antagonism in all quarters.

President John F. Kennedy went even further than Eisenhower in changing the relationship between the President and the press and public. He brought an element of showmanship to the White House by initiating the live televised press conference. The intention, of course, was to give the government and particularly the President greater visibility with the American people.

Unfortunately, the quality of the press conference as a device for eliciting information about government was not improved by its live telecast. The presidential press conference show, along with the interview and talk programs that became a mainstay of radio and television public service, brought about the change in the newspaper business that caused the star system to spread. Big money earnings were no longer uncommon among newsmen; they brought with them tangible evidence of the importance of the newsmen, and self-importance brought a lessening of humility and humor in relations between the government and the fourth estate. This, in turn, created new frictions.

Kennedy, like most of the Presidents before him, beginning with George Washington, fought with the press. He cancelled the White House subscriptions to the New York *Herald Tribune*, a Republican newspaper that was critical of him. His aides lied to the press on the Bay of Pigs affair, when the U.S. government supported the efforts of Cuban refugees to invade Cuba, and the CIA supplied arms and transportation. That gave the press cause to complain that security was being used to cover up government mistakes, and the credibility gap between governors and governed widened.

President Lyndon B. Johnson disliked the televised presidential press conference because he knew he was not good at it. He operated as he had when a senator, in an atmosphere of secrecy and indirection. As noted in an earlier chapter he made a serious attempt to manipulate the press regarding the war in Vietnam. The press came to distrust him completely, and so did the public to a large extent, over the issue of the war. The credibility gap increased so seriously that Johnson began to doubt his chances of reelection in 1968, and as a result he chose not to run again for the Presidency.

By the time President Richard M. Nixon took office, the tensions between the reporters and the White House were very severe. Nixon's relative unpopularity with reporters in general did not help matters. But on the other hand, the problems of the Presidency and of American government that President Nixon faced really surmounted personality and any President's relationship with the press. There had been so many changes, some of them obvious, some of them subtle, that old relationships could no longer exist.

One basic change was in the very size of the operations of government. Government grew, but press coverage really did not grow to match it. Newhouse newspapers, for example, maintained some twenty-four reporters in Washington, but was that adequate coverage for the most powerful newspaper chain in the country? Knight newspapers maintained over a dozen reporters there, but was that enough? *The New York Times,* which claimed to cover all the news, had around fifty Washington reporters. The New York *Journal of Commerce* had more reporters in Washington than Newhouse did. The Denver *Post*, the Dallas *Morning News*, and many other big regional newspapers had no more than two or three Washington reporters—no more than the Eugene *Register-Guard*, a little newspaper in a relatively small Oregon city. The Honolulu *Star-Bulletin* had only one reporter in Washington.

Of course freedom of the press in the United States was not a Washington affair alone. But as matters were developing in America, freedom of the news media was basically an affair between the media and the federal government. In the final analysis, no matter what pressures were exerted by local authority or what state laws might be passed to restrict people or ideas, the case would come before the federal courts and ultimately the United States Supreme Court because of the all-embracing nature of the First Amendment to the Constitution. And what could be said about Washington, in regard to government and reportorial initiative, could be said about every state house and state legislature in the land. The press simply did not keep up with the coverage of government.

The networks seemed more impressive than the print news services, until it was realized that the number of actual correspondents was relatively much smaller, and that these were split between radio and television. Considering the number of reporters and the vast nature of government, even if information was easily available and there were no problems of secrecy, it was not surprising that government was covered no better than it was. And the fact that the news media were deep in recession in the early seventies did not help. As advertising revenue declined, both newspapers and networks were firing rather than hiring reporters.

During President Nixon's first term in office, it was not the President himself, but Vice President Spiro T. Agnew who was at the center of the most significant controversy regarding freedom of the media. In several widely publicized speeches, Agnew charged that important segments of the press had shown serious bias against the Nixon administration and were reporting the news neither properly nor accurately. The reaction of the news media was a mixture of injured pride and real fear on the parts of some that Spiro Agnew was beginning an administration vendetta against the press that might lead to restrictions on press freedom.

Distrust between the press and the Nixon administration

was occasioned by many factors. For one thing, administration officials felt they were mistreated by the press, that the press did not protect their privacy in off-the-record conversations. Over the years newspapermen and other journalists had welcomed the "briefing" or "backgrounder" in which a high government official would tell the press the inside story on an event or situation, but not for direct quotation. Newsmen began to break this rule, and the Washington *Post* flouted it openly one day in the case of Dr. Henry Kissinger. As John P. Roche, once a State Department spokesman and later a columnist, put it, the "leak" or authorized use of classified information for attribution as to material but not source, was one thing. But the violation of confidence was another.

The American press seemed to be singularly blind to the realities of government's responsibilities: that a government must govern, as well as reveal information. Certain things, defense matters, foreign relations in particular, had always been conducted in relative secrecy. Violations of confidence by the press could hurt no one more than the press. The administration after the Nixon administration would be more careful to avoid situations of this kind—and more care meant less freedom of access by newsmen to government sources.

Yet, by midsummer of 1972 the Nixon administration had actually done what previous administrations had only talked of doing. The number of persons permitted to classify government documents secret and above had been decreased by 63 per cent. A special commission headed by John Eisenhower, son of the late President, was investigating and trying to cut down even further on this spate of secret paper that glutted the channels of government. It is doubtful that so much would have been accomplished so quickly had not the effort been spurred by the embarrassments of the months just before in the matter of the Pentagon Papers and the India-Pakistan crisis.

Since the founding of the Republic, it was always obvious that there would be conflict between the fourth estate and "duly-constituted authority"; it was acknowledged that such conflict actually worked in the interest of the nation. A free and responsible press was important to keep government in line. But along with freedom came responsibility. In the 1970s the media's negligence of their responsibility to report the news accurately, fairly, objectively was becoming of rising government and public concern. It was also of concern to many news-media people. When 75 per cent of the members of Congress without regard to party, said they thought TV news was biased, they might not all be talking about the same thing, but they had a feeling that television presentations were not telling the real story.

There were some real threats to freedom of the press on the part of government, and this was also a public concern. The major threats involved the subpoena of the notes and files of journalists and publications, court rulings that newsmen did not have the right to protect sources, and the impersonation of newsmen by police officials.

The news media believed, too, that the complaints of Vice President Agnew were a threat to press freedom. Yet Agnew must have his freedom under the First Amendment just as much as the press. (Testifying before a Congressional committee on the "intimidation" of the press by Vice President Agnew, David Brinkley remarked in typical Brinkley fashion that he did not notice anybody being visibly intimidated.)

The press also saw a threat to its freedom in the refusal of officials to meet with press representatives whose media had opposed the officials. Such action on the part of the officials might be foolish policy, but it did not impinge on the right of the people to know.

Freedom of the press did not mean—as some newsmen seemed to think it did—that officials or others were bound to love or even respect any segment of the press. But then, neither was it ever incumbent on the news media people to love or even respect any segment of the government. The members of each side would have love or respect as they deserved it; such matters could not be guaranteed. All that could be guaranteed was the right of the media to investigate and print the findings without any more restraint than would be imposed on any citizen.

Freedom of the press did not mean the freedom to libel or to commit any unlawful act; newsmen and media had to be responsible for their actions. If they stole documents, and printed the documents, they might be prosecuted under laws dealing with theft.

But the moves to limit sources were definite threats to long-range freedom. In 1970 federal authorities subpoenaed tapes and out-takes of a CBS documentary on the Black Panther movement. That same year authorities subpoenaed files and pictures of *Time*, *Life*, and *Newsweek* dealing with the Weathermen, the violent faction of the Students for a Democratic Society. A federal prosecutor subpoenaed Earl Caldwell, reporter for *The New York Times*, demanding his testimony and his notes on the Black Panthers. In each of these cases, the government was looking into organizations that allegedly were seditious or even treasonous.

The principal offender in all this was the United States Department of Justice. Its prosecutors subpoenaed newsmen in various parts of the country: Missouri, Maryland, Kentucky, Delaware, Wisconsin. The press resisted in every case, and there were hundreds of cases. Three of them became very important and went to the United States Supreme Court. They were the Caldwell case and two others: a case involving Paul M. Branzburg, a reporter for the Detroit *Free Press* and a former reporter of the Louisville *Courier-Journal,* and the case of Paul Pappas, a reporter-cameraman for WTEV-TV of New Bedford, Massachusetts.

Paul Branzburg was called before a county grand jury in 1969 after he wrote an article for the Louisville *Courier-Journal* in which he told about watching two men make hashish. He was asked to identify the men, refused, and was charged with contempt. The case was appealed and eventually reached the Supreme Court, which ruled that Branzburg had to answer the questions. He was sentenced to six months in jail.

Paul Pappas spent a night with the Black Panthers in their headquarters during disturbances in 1970. He was subpoenaed to testify, refused, and was held in contempt. The case reached the Supreme Court, and in the summer of 1972 the court held that newsmen, like other citizens, had to testify in criminal investigations. The decision was 5 to 4, with Justice White writing the majority report. "The Constitution does not, as it never has, exempt the newsman from performing the citizen's normal duty of appearing and furnishing information relevant to the grand jury's task," he said. White's point was that the newsman is not free to publish whatever he wants without being called to account for it. For example, he said, there were libel laws, and newsmen were denied access to certain meetings and procedures.

However, the 5 to 4 decision meant there was a large body of opinion, represented in the court, that held quite differently. Justice Potter Stewart said the ruling "invites state and federal authorities to undermine the historic independence of the press by attempting to annex the journalistic profession as an investigative arm of the government."

Certainly there was room for argument. It did not seem right that a criminal should go free simply because a reporter refused to divulge information. And yet, by calling attention to the situation in the first place (as in the Branzburg case), the reporter showed authority where government was falling down. If the world at large knew that reporters could not protect their sources, many people would not talk to reporters at all, and many certainly would not talk as freely as they might otherwise.

It was always part of a reporter's credo that he could not be forced to reveal his source of information, and in 1972 eighteen states had shield laws that protected the reporter in this regard. The decision of the Supreme Court in the Pappas case probably made most of them no longer applicable, however, and opened the press to a severe trial of its ability to retain its independence.

What could happen was shown in the case of John Kifner, a reporter for *The New York Times*, covering the 1969 convention of the Students for a Democratic Society. Previously, Anthony Ripley, another *Times* reporter, had testified under subpoena about the SDS before the Internal Security Committee of the House of Representatives. As a result the SDS had barred all members of the "capitalist press" from their convention. Mr. Kifner found it very hard to cover the activities of the SDS in view of the change. The radicals simply did not trust any reporters, based on their experience.

The government has remedy: if it discovers the source of leaks, the "leak" can be prosecuted. Perhaps one very good solution would be the passage of an official secrets law such as the one that exists in Great Britain. Under that law, persons in position of trust understand from the moment they take that trust that it is binding, and that if they divulge secret in-

formation at any time, they not only run the risk of prosecu-
tion, but almost certainly will be prosecuted. The leaks in
Britain are fewer than the leaks in America, and the press in
Britain retains its freedom.

A very serious threat to the freedom of the press in the
1970s was the law officers' practice of impersonating newsmen. In Saigon in 1970 four government agents masquer-
aded as members of the press corps for two weeks to try to
discover the sources of the real newsmen. It was not an
isolated case, as the media learned. Army agents had been
using this "cover" since 1967, and other police agencies were
doing it, too. For some other examples: In 1967 a photographer for the Spanish-language paper *El Tiempo* was working
as a federal agent. Carl Gilman, a TV reporter for San
Diego's KFMB-TV, was a paid FBI informer. The Army's security agency used informants posing as newsmen to "cover"
the 1968 Democratic convention in Chicago. The Washington police used a woman agent who posed as a reporter.
There were dozens of other cases across the nation.

Obviously this was dangerous to freedom of the press, but
there was an obvious remedy for it: publicity. Each time one
of these undercover agents was exposed by the media, not
only was the "cover" broken, but the public knew what was
happening. The agencies involved never really tried to defend this practice, although no government agency was very
quick to condemn it either. One of the realities of the 1970s
was that the world was full of spies—one huge agency of the
United States government, the CIA, was totally dedicated to
espionage. Given acceptance of the espionage state, which
seemed to persist through administration after administration, then it was naive to believe that such a cover as that of
reporter would never be used again by government agents.

The cover was just too good—who had a better right to be out snooping around than a reporter? No, the use of agents posing as newsmen was something that would go on—but what was important was the attitude taken by the press toward such a practice. In the case of the Washington policewoman who posed as a newswoman, the reporters of the Washington *Star* responded in just the right way—they protested the police policy and pledged themselves to unmask any undercover police agent posing as a newsperson in the future. There was their real protection.

Another serious threat to the freedom of the press, and one considered quite important by the task force of the Twentieth Century Fund, was the failure of the general press to support and protect the underground press from government harassment, which was noted in an earlier chapter. Obviously this threat was real—for what could apply to the underground press one day, could apply to all the press, all the media of information, the next day. The price of liberty was still, in the 1970s, unceasing vigilance.

Certainly the press and government must remain at arms' length. This was not true in other countries, however. In France, for example, the newspapers in 1972 took $3 million in assistance as subsidy from the French government. The newspapers had their troubles, the number was down in the national capital from thirty-two just after World War II to eleven in 1972; advertising revenues were off 20 per cent and newspapers were suffering badly. The competition of television again. But a direct subsidy? Very questionable practice, particularly in view of the history of the French press, which was in the pay of many forces, especially the Nazis, just before World War II, and whose defection from the cause of liberty was credited with many of France's ills in those years.

When one adds the situation in the French press to the

fact that French radio and television are also controlled by the government to a very large extent (in 1972 the French government fired the leading director of French television because of his public affairs probing), then one can see that French media are not free in the American sense. They could not be counted on to resist the government if they—and that means a number of people—felt it necessary.

No one to whom freedom is a credo would advocate a similar system for the United States.

EPILOGUE

In the 1970s, freedom of the media involved many things, and some of the most important aspects of the issue were the least popular. In the summer of 1972 came a perfect example of this truth:

In Georgia, J. B. Stoner, a candidate for the United States Senate, ran for office on an unabashed program of racism. He referred in his advertising and his speeches to "niggers" and claimed that you could not "have law and order and niggers too. Vote white."

The NAACP and various other organizations were aghast and sought control of this advertising by the Federal Communications Commission, since it appeared on television. But the FCC ruled against interfering with the advertisements. No matter how offensive they might be to blacks or nonblacks, the ads did not incite to riot or advocate violence. The ads represented a point of view that most Americans found offensive, but the FCC was quite right in refusing to interfere, in allowing the racist candidate to say what he wished, as long as he did not break any laws. That was precisely what freedom of the media was all about—the freedom to express unpopular, even abhorrent ideas.

In the 1970s, there were many legitimate problems of freedom. There was the case of Daniel Schorr, a CBS correspondent in Washington, for instance. Schorr was not really regarded as a friend of the Nixon administration; indeed the Washington *Post* described him in a headline as a "critical newsman." Suddenly Schorr found himself the subject of an FBI investigation. He protested to the White House and was told that he was under consideration for an important administration post. This was most unlikely, given Schorr's natural leanings and the attitude he had shown toward the Nixon administration.

Schorr and other newsmen regarded the matter as a case of attempted intimidation. Was it? It was harassment, but probably it did not intimidate Schorr. Most important, when it was exposed, the harassment ceased—and that was the best possible solution to the problem. Newspapers and editorialists elsewhere raged against the government's action and beat their breasts in behalf of freedom of the press, of course—and thus proved that the press was indeed free to do just that, which was very important to know.

In the spring of 1972, Bill Monroe, an NBC newsman and editor, said that the press was complacent and shameful for letting government erode its areas of freedom. If that was true early in 1972, it was not true by the middle of the year. The press was far from complacent, it was complaining all over the place. Monroe himself tried to put the blame on government for the timidity of broadcast journalism, and the blame on newspapers for not standing up for the absolute freedom (from FCC control) that the broadcasters wanted.

Yet in spite of the plaints of Monroe and others, one reality did stand out in 1973: there was no such thing as absolute freedom and there could never be absolute freedom. The question once again was the one raised years ago by Mr. Justice Holmes: Has a man the right to cry "fire" in a crowded theater?

In the 1970s, the erosion of all areas of the individual's

personal freedom was continuing. There would have to be new compromises, and there might have to be changes made in the laws concerning violation of confidence and secrets of the federal government. It was a harsh world, a fast-moving world, where conceivably the violations of confidence of an individual, coming at the wrong time, could cost *all the nation all its freedoms.* In the 1970s that had to be considered, and it had not been, really. No one had ever attempted to assess, for example, the cost of the Chicago *Tribune*'s dishonorable exposure of the American success in breaking the Japanese codes during World War II. That certainly could not be justified by "freedom of the press."

In 1972 the American Society of Newspaper Editors complained that there was more government hostility to the press on every level than there had been previously. Of course there would be—and the hostility indicated that the press was doing its job. The ASNE was also concerned about growing attempts by government to preserve its secrets from the eyes of the press and the public. But government would always attempt to keep its secrets, newsmen would always attempt to uncover them, and the existence of the tension and the conflict guaranteed freedom of the press and better government for all.

There would always be threats to freedom of the press as long as power was placed in the hands of persons who believed their immediate duties and actions were all-important. The press existed to keep track of just such people, to inform the public of the activities of government.

The ills were seen in different lights by the various factions. Government people, like former Secretary of Commerce Maurice Stans, could quite conscientiously accuse the press of distortion when it charged him with conflict of interest, after he had given a full statement to the press on his financial holdings. Nixon Press Secretary Ron Ziegler could complain that the press identified Henry Kissinger in a background briefing story, when it had always been tacitly understood that the press would not do this. The press could quite conscientiously accuse the government of tightening its reins and of trying to manipulate the news media.

These things were actually happening. That most of them did not represent basic threats to government function or to freedom of the news media was indicated by all the publicity all of them received, by the serious mien the United States Supreme Court turned toward the problems of press freedom at all times, by the delay even in the trial of admitted "leaker" Daniel Ellsberg when it seemed his rights might have been violated.

Ralph Nader urged the establishment of a Center for Journalistic Policy, to make the news media more responsive to the consumer. At the end of 1972, the Twentieth Century Fund created such a press council (with no coercive powers) in spite of the overwhelming opposition of the American Society of Newspaper Editors. "I don't think it will work," said Benjamin Bradlee, executive editor of the Washington *Post*.

Similar ideas had been urged before—but was such a center, or police force, needed? Government and the law policed the press, just as the press policed government. These were normal functions, and they were functioning normally in the early 1970s.

The threat to freedom is compounded by the fear that the protests of the minorities engender in the hearts of business-oriented newspaper executives. One should expect more from the persons of power who are in control of newspapers, but the tendency of wealth is to protect wealth. Consequently the answers to the problems of minority hiring and minority reporting must come from within the profession of journalism, not from outside it. Whether the answers can come quickly enough will influence the future course of the freedom of the media very heavily.

If the newspapers and the journalism schools could convince the minority groups by action of their determination to wipe out old evils, the situation would be vastly improved. But if it came to the arbitrary imposition of quotas and minority hiring at the expense of the middle class, then there would be trouble aplenty. All this adds up to problems of trust and distrust, one of the prime internal threats to freedom of the news media in the 1970s.

More important is the fourth-estate tradition of objectivity—the basic idea, under fire in the 1970s from the new journalism, that an honest reporter can tell the facts of a situation in an unbiased report, no matter how he feels about the matter personally, and an honest editor, reading the reporter's copy, can help the reporter to do this and overcome any shortcomings, without regard to the editor's own bias. To deny that all persons have bias would be foolish; to deny that professional journalists cannot overcome bias, would be to deny the whole basis of freedom, or the viability of a general newspaper. As A. J. Liebling once said: "There is a healthy American newspaper tradition of not taking yourself seriously. It is the story you must take that way."

There were threats to freedom of the news media in the 1970s, both internal and external, but the Supreme Court had shown decisively its concern for the First Amendment. By and large the news media in the United States were free, and they would continue to enjoy their freedom, just as long as they wanted freedom enough to work for it.

BIBLIOGRAPHY

Barnouw, Erik. *A History of Broadcasting in the United States.* Vol. I (To 1933): *A Tower in Babel.* New York: Oxford University Press, Inc., 1966.

———. Vol. 2 (1933-53): *The Golden Web.* 1968.

———. Vol. 3 (From 1953): *The Image Empire.* 1970.

Bird, George, and Frederic Merwin, eds. *Press and Society: A Book of Readings.* New York: Prentice-Hall, Inc., 1951.

Efron, Edith. *The News Twisters.* Los Angeles: Nash Publishing Corp., 1971.

Keogh, James. *President Nixon and the Press.* New York: Funk and Wagnalls, Inc., 1972.

Markel, Lester. *What You Don't Know Can Hurt You.* Washington, D.C.: Public Affairs Press, 1972.

Mayer, Martin. *About Television.* New York: Harper & Row, Publishers, 1972.

Mott, Frank Luther. *A History of American Magazines,* 5 vols. (1741-1930). Cambridge: Harvard University Press, 1968.

———. *American Journalism.* New York: The Macmillan Company, 1972.

The Twentieth Century Fund. *Press Freedoms Under Pressure.* New York, 1972.

In the preparation of this book, the authors consulted the files of *Life, Newsweek, Time,* and many other magazines. Newspapers studied included *The New York Times,* Washington *Evening Star-News,* Washington *Post.* The authors also drew on their own experiences with the media, including the Colorado Springs *Free Press,* Colorado Springs *News,* Denver *Post,* Portland *Oregonian,* San Francisco *Chronicle,* Washington *Evening Star, American Heritage, Collier's, Time,* United Press Associations, and CBS News.

INDEX